The Girls He Left Behind

Barbara June Jackson

First published on Amazon in 2023

Copyright© Barbara June Jackson

All rights reserved. No part of this publication may be reproduced, stored in a retrieval system or transmitted, in any form or by any means without the prior written permission of the publisher, nor be otherwise circulated in any form of binding or cover other than that in which it is published and without a similar condition being imposed on the subsequent purchaser.

Paperback ISBN: 9798377248903

All reasonable steps have been taken to ensure that details in the book are as accurate as possible. However, in the words of our late Queen, recollections may vary.

In memory of Leonora Knatchbull, Sean Robb and all the beautiful young children who have lost their lives from cancer.

All proceeds from THE GIRLS HE LEFT BEHIND will be donated to the THE EDWINA MOUNTBATTEN AND LEONORA CHILDREN'S FOUNDATION.
This is a registered charity which supports the following:

Nurses caring for children suffering with cancer

The furtherance of primary research into causes of paediatric cancers.

The relief of sick, distressed or needy children in any part of the world.

This book is dedicated to my Father and all those brave servicemen and women,
in both World Wars, who gave their lives fighting for their country.

Introduction

The year was 1938, German troops were massing on the border of Czechoslovakia, and the spectre of war was looming. At the heart of the problem was Adolph Hitler's determination to unite his country by annexing the province of Sudetenland, home to over three million ethnic German people.

On September 30th, at a conference in Munich, the German Chancellor categorically assured the British and Italian Prime Ministers, Neville Chamberlain and Benito Mussolini, and the President of France, Edouard Daladier, that the annexation of the Czech province would be his only territorial claim in Europe. The four heads of state then signed the Munich agreement, and for the time being, the threat of war was averted.

Prime Minister Chamberlain was met by cheering crowds and photographers when he flew into Heston Aerodrome after the conference. Proudly flourishing a piece of paper bearing the signatures of himself and Hitler, he triumphantly proclaimed there was to be "Peace in our Time."

On September 1st 1939, despite the Fuhrer's guarantee he would make no more territorial claims, the armed forces of the Third Reich invaded Poland, thus triggering the start of World War II. Two days later, on September 3rd, Great Britain declared war on Germany.

This short, illustrated book follows the story of my father, Ronald Frank Millard Adams, from Wickham in Hampshire, and the other 156,000 brave soldiers, who sailed to France on June 6th 1944, to fight for their country.

Chapter 1

On June 28th 1914, the assassinations in Sarajevo of the heir to the Austro-Hungarian Empire, Archduke Franz Ferdinand and his wife Sophie set off a chain of events that led to the First World War. It was a violent conflict which lasted four years, destabilised Europe and resulted in many millions of lives being lost.

Ronald's father, Millard was born in 1895 to Fareham Forestry worker William George Adams and his wife, Annie, who came from the nearby village of Soberton. He joined the Royal Regiment of Artillery after being called up to fight in November 1915 and on March 8th 1916, he left England to join the British troops fighting in France. The location of his first posting is unknown, but on August 29th of that same year, army records show he was sent to the "battle in the field."

Land warfare was hellish for the troops in the muddy, rat-infested, unsanitary trenches, where they had to endure the constant threat of bullets, shell fire and gas attacks, plus the additional fear of falling victim to the often fatal diseases of dysentery, typhoid, cholera and influenza.

Field service postcards, with various options printed on them, were a means of communication for soldiers and their loved ones and on September 18th 1918, Millard sent one to his girlfriend Rose with all options crossed out except "I am quite well." She was delighted to receive it and to know, at least for the time being, the man she loved was alive and uninjured.

Millard's WWI Regimental Photograph

Field Service Postcard Sent from Millard to Rose 1918

Millard's WWI medals

On November 11th 1918, the war finally ended and on January 24th 1919, Millard sailed with his regiment from the French port of Dunkirk back to Dover. After he returned home it was apparent to his family and friends that his years on the battlefield had affected him deeply. However, over the years he regained his health and strength and on a snowy Boxing Day morning in 1923, in St Peter and St Paul's Church, Fareham, he married Rosina, the daughter of Frank and Elizabeth Day. Just over a year later, on March 2nd 1925, their son Ronald, my father, was born.

Millard had always aspired to be a market gardener, and as soon as circumstances allowed, he bought an eight-acre plot of land on the outskirts of Wickham, a village in Hampshire.

Rose and Millard's Wedding

Rose, Millard and Ronald at their farm 1927

At the beginning life was tough for the young couple but they worked hard and eventually the business prospered. They derived great joy from their baby and later, when he was a toddler, were constantly amused by his antics. As the years passed, Rose would feel a deep sense of pride when she watched him and his father, dressed identically in traditional leather gaiters, set off for work after enjoying a breakfast she had lovingly cooked for them.

Ronald proved to be a capable farmhand, tackling every job he was given enthusiastically. However, he was never happier than when helping groom their workhorse, Hercules; the patient, plodding dobbin would stand as still as a statue while he and his father rigorously cleaned him up and brushed him until his coat shone. Then, at the end of each day, they'd carefully check him over for cuts, swellings, loose horseshoes and any other workhorse-related problems that may have befallen him.

Millard's land was on the Strawberry Coast, an area in the county of Hampshire encompassing the fertile Hamble valley where the deep, rich sandy loam soil was and still is perfect for strawberry growing. Over the years, their cultivation proved commercially profitable for him and other farmers and market gardeners. The harvesting of strawberries usually began in June when the fruit was picked and put into large wicker containers called gallons, made by the inmates of Winchester jail. When they were full, they would be loaded onto carts and transported to various train stations. On arrival, they'd be packed onto "Strawberry Specials" and whisked off to Covent Garden and other destinations nationwide. A new station, specially built for the expanding Hampshire strawberry industry, was opened on September 2nd 1889; oddly enough, despite being closer to the village of Park Gate, it was called Swanwick and, for the duration of the harvest, was one of the busiest stations in the country.

Picking strawberries is backbreaking work, and farmers were grateful when the gypsies and other seasonal agricultural workers appeared. They were also delighted when local children were given special dispensation to take time off school and allowed to become part of the workforce.

Chapter 2

Wickham, where our story begins, is a village in Hampshire steeped in history. Once a Saxon settlement and a Roman military post, it was mentioned in the Royal Charter of 826AD. Later, in the Domesday Book, Britain's earliest public record, it was noted as having a population of 120 and two water mills.

This picturesque location is ideally situated in rolling downland on the edge of the scenic Meon Valley, with water meadows nearby offering an escape from the hustle and bustle of modern life. The villages' medieval square, the second largest in England, is graced with many elegant and imposing ivy-clad 16th, 17th and 18th-century houses. In Bridge Street, which connects the village to the church via the north ford, there are three picturesque timber-framed cottages dating back to 1495, called The Old Barracks. Rumour has it that Queen Anne or Queen Elizabeth I's guards were once billeted in them while the Monarch, on a visit to the area, stayed conveniently nearby in a 17th-century house called Queen's Lodge.

An imposing building called Chesapeake Mill is situated further along the street. It was built in 1820 using American white oak salvaged from the frigate USS Chesapeake, captured in 1813 during the war between Great Britain and America. It was a working watermill until 1976 and is now a Grade II listed property containing shops full of traditional and vintage lifestyle accessories, plus an excellent range of products for homes and gardens. There is also a traditional tearoom called Crumbs, where, as the River Meon flows sedately by, you can relax after shopping

F. S. CLARK

General and Fancy Draper,

Wickham, Hants.

28th August, 1944.

Dear Sir or Madam,

I beg to inform you that Jean Iris Potter (Miss) of "Woodstock" Church Road, Titchfield Common, Fareham, has been in my employ since 7th July 1941, terminating on her own request the 26th August 1944.

Miss Potter came as an apprentice, to attain the position as a first hand saleswoman, gaining a favorable knowledge throughout the Drapery Trade.

I have found her capabilities all that can be desired. Honest above all. Reliable, hardworking, and a pleasing manner.

I have no hesitation in recommending Miss Potter to any branch of salesmanship within her scope.

Yours truly,

sgd F.S.CLARK

Proprietor

Letter of reference

to enjoy a refreshing pot of tea and delicious cakes.

Another striking Grade II listed building stands on Clark's corner at the top of the Square. In the late 1800s, it housed a haberdashery store run by three sisters and their nephews, and later, when taken over by Mr F. W. Clark in 1897, it became "Clark's Drapers and Outfitters." The shop held a grand summer sale in 1909, which no doubt in those days would have been a significant village event, and on the day, there were fireworks and a brass band to entertain the shoppers. When my mother left school in 1940, she worked as a shop assistant in this store and I have a letter of reference written by the Proprietor, Mr. F. S. Clark, which describes her in the following words: "I have found her capabilities all that can be desired. Honest above all, reliable, hardworking, and a pleasing manner."

A special event for which Wickham is famous is its Horse Fair, held in the village since 1269. It was initially opened by a horse, name unknown, while supping its first drink at the Star Inn; not surprisingly, that tradition died out over the years. Thousands of people come from far and wide to trade horses, participate in races and celebrate reuniting with family and friends. The Fair has always been especially popular with Romany families who, on the day, would make spectacular entrances into the village in their beautifully painted caravans but, by tradition, would not be allowed into the Square until St Nicholas's church clock struck noon. A funfair with carousels, shooting galleries, and candy floss stalls is always part of this event, attracting old and young alike. It is not surprising the Wickham Horse Fair is still a very popular event almost 800 years after it began.

William of Wykeham was the village's most famous son. Born in 1320, he was Lord Chancellor of England to Edward III and Richard II. He founded Winchester College whose pupils are known as Wykamists. This academic institution is considered among the most prestigious in the world and its former alumni include many well-known literary, political and sporting figures. Those educated within its hallowed walls include six previous Chancellors of the Exchequer, many high-ranking military officers, several famous authors and our present Prime Minister Rishi Sunak.

A splendid 12th-century church dedicated to St Nicholas stands east of the River Meon. Inside, on one wall is a 20th-century oak screen in memory of those who lost their lives in World War 1 and on another, a Hopton stone tablet commemorating the 12 parishioners who died in World War II.

My father was baptised in this ancient place of worship on June 7th 1925 and his name appears on the stone tablet inside the church and also on the plinth of the impressive War Memorial that stands in the churchyard.

.

Chapter 3

Ronald occasionally accompanied his father on shopping trips to the village however, on the occasions he left his son at home, Millard would drop into the King's Head, a former coaching inn named after Henry III. The atmosphere in the pub in those days was particularly convivial as the bars were filled with agricultural workers drinking well-earned pints and playing darts, dominoes and cards. Millard occasionally joined them as he liked nothing better than a game of five-card brag and a glass of excellent Gales ale brewed in Horndean, just 16 miles away.

As a market gardener, Millard needed to control the pests on his land. Birds were his worst nightmare, especially magpies, blue tits and finches; in winter, they'd steal the dormant buds from the trees in his orchard and, in summer, strip the ripe fruit from them. So he decided to drape netting over the trees, but the "damned feathered nuisances," as he called them, still ingeniously found their way through it. The other deterrent he employed was an old shotgun which he'd discharge to frighten them off, but that didn't always work, as they felt bold enough to return the minute he stopped firing.

On his son's 14th birthday, Millard took him into Hundred Acres Wood, opposite them, to teach him the rudiments of shooting. Much to his father's surprise, Ronald bagged a grey squirrel with his first shot; four years later, its fluffy tail, which he kept for luck, would go with him when he sailed to the beaches of Normandy.

The time eventually came for Millard and Rose to replace their old home, and my father, I was told, laid the first stone of their new three-bedroom house. It was surrounded by gardens that looked bare in winter. However, as soon as spring arrived, snowdrops, primroses and crocuses would miraculously burst through the cold, hard earth, followed by golden daffodils and multicoloured tulips. Later in summer, beds of roses would provide a colourful, eye-catching display, while those planted with sweet-smelling lavender, honeysuckle and jasmine not only looked beautiful but filled the air with fragrance. Fir trees lined the back of the garden, and, in front of them, there was a charming arbour covered in lavender-blue wisteria where I would sit with my grandmother while she read to me from the book of Hans Christian Anderson's Fairy Tales. An ornamental fishpond, set in the middle of the lawn, with giant water lilies floating on it, was home to an enormous white goldfish that would swim around, safely hidden by the lilies' bright green leaves. There were

always herons flying around the area, and it was nothing short of a miracle that, for almost 30 years, the goldfish managed to avoid being snatched by one of those rapacious birds. Finally, shading the pond was a laburnum tree with golden chains of pendulous flowers. It was always lovely when in bloom, but I was warned never to eat the poisonous seed pods it shed.
.

The house itself had a delightful aspect, and on a fine day, the sitting room would be bathed in soft, glowing sunlight. A black ebony piano stood in one corner, and Rose loved bashing out medleys of popular songs on its well-worn keys. She would also entertain her guests with tunes on the piano accordion, mandolin, ukulele and banjo; an incredible achievement as, unable to read music, she played all the instruments by ear.

There was a bright, colourful kitchen with a window overlooking the rear garden at the back of the house. Rose was an excellent cook, and the intoxicating and pungent smell of spices, which hit you as soon as you opened the back door, permeated the air. Curiously, she cooked everything with local homemade butter bought from a neighbour she called "The Colonel;" it was nice and creamy, although I thought it tasted a bit like cheese rind. She produced great roast dinners, but her forte was baking cakes, and her cherry, coconut and Madeira ones were so delicious that my father and grandfather frequently devoured them before they had even cooled down.

There were three bedrooms and a bathroom on the upstairs floor of the house, providing plenty of sleeping accommodation for the three of them. I remember the back bedroom, where I always slept on my childhood visits, had an

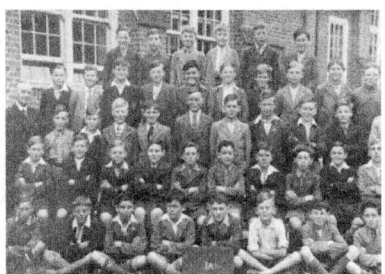

2nd row 6th from left

Football team - top row 2nd from right

Ronalds schooldays

excellent view of Portsdown Hill on a clear day.

Photographs of my father show him with a cheeky grin and, in primary school, according to his mother, he was popular with his classmates. In the playground, he and his friends enjoyed playing a game which involved attaching large brown seeds to long pieces of string. The seeds, called conkers, came from the horse chestnut tree and the boys would swing them around with great force; it was nothing short of a miracle they didn't sustain nasty injuries to their knuckles or even their heads. They also loved playing that age-old game of knocking the ball around and frequently ended up with scraped knees and bruises after falling onto the playground's hard, unforgiving surface. Meanwhile, the ladylike young girls, hair neatly arranged in plaits, pigtails or ponytails, enjoyed more gentle pursuits, like hopscotch and skipping.

When he was 11, Ronald became a pupil at Fareham Secondary School for boys. Although intelligent, he was not academic, but he loved sport, and one of his proudest moments was being picked to play for his school's football team. It's believed a silver trophy which is now one of my treasured possessions was won by him in the 1938/39 Hampshire Junior Schools Football competition.

The family often took lunch together in the rear garden. It was an idyllic spot, and, at certain times of the year, they could enjoy the scent of honeysuckle and jasmine as it mingled with the delicate aroma of the fruit tree blossom drifting up from the orchard.

Hundred Acres was a happy home for them. However, at 11.15 am on Sunday,

September 3rd 1939, Ronald, Rose and Millard, along with most people in Great Britain, listened, on their respective radios, to the declaration of war by Prime Minister Neville Chamberlain; he said:

"I am speaking to you from the cabinet room at 10 Downing Street. This morning the British ambassador in Berlin handed the German Government a final note stating that unless we heard from them by eleven o'clock that they were prepared at once to withdraw their troops from Poland, a state of war would exist between us. I have to tell you now that no such undertaking has been received and that consequently, this country is at war with Germany."

My father would have listened attentively and, no doubt, wished he was old enough to fight.

Chapter 4

In 1925, in the city of Portsmouth, a young man called William Potter married a pretty young lady called Violet Budden. A year later, on June 24th 1926, their daughter Joan, my mother, came into the world.

William's father was a Royal Navy Officer from the village of Kentisbeare in Devon who, in 1894, married a widow from Portsmouth called Alice with three children. My grandfather, William was born when they went on to have a family of their own.

Violet's father, Louis Richard Budden, an acting sergeant in the Worcester regiment in World War 1, married his wife, Ida, in 1898 and Violet had two brothers and a sister. She was a bright child who excelled at arithmetic and, even at 80 years old,

A family wedding with Joan's parents and Grandparents and her Aunt Doris in attendance

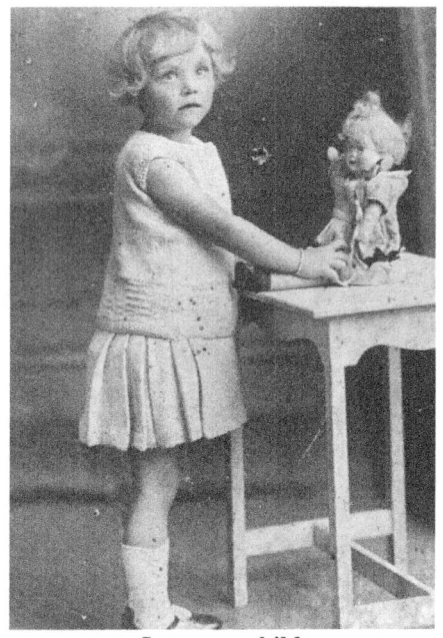

Joan as a child

Joan in 1939

could add up a column of figures quicker than it takes a teenager of today to pick up a calculator. On leaving school, she became a cashier at Handley's, a prestigious store in the seaside resort of Southsea. Some years later, after she and William were married, she gave birth to my mother, Joan, with two more children, Alan and Doris, following in quick succession. One winter, the two little girls became very ill with double pneumonia, an infection often fatal in young children in the 1930s. Joan survived, but Doris, to the deep sorrow of her parents, died.

Their son, Alan, thankfully did not fall victim to the disease and in 1946 left home and joined the Royal Navy. He spent much of his life in the Senior Service as a submariner after being an Apprentice Artificer at HMS Fisgard, a Royal Naval Training Establishment at Torpoint in Cornwall. Later he served as a Chief Petty

Officer, Engine Room Artificer on the diesel submarines HMS Trespasser and HMS Seneschal.

On a trip in the early 50s, his ship called into the port of Colombo in Sri Lanka, and there he met and fell in love with his future wife, a fiercely proud Cornish girl named Oonagh. After a two-week whirlwind courtship and on receiving a positive response for her hand from her stepfather, Alan proposed. He carefully slipped a deep blue Ceylonese sapphire ring onto her finger then unceremoniously dispatched her to England to live with us in Locksheath. Although I was very young at the time, I remember her arriving at the house wearing a donkey brown coat with just 10 shillings in her pocket. I adored her at first sight, and she fitted in perfectly with us all, becoming another daughter for my grandparents, a good friend to my Mother and a very special Aunt to me.

Oonagh, originally coming from the magical county of Cornwall with its mysterious Arthurian legends, was like someone exotic coming into our rather dull lives. She would hold us spellbound for hours with exciting stories that could have come straight from the pages of a Poldark novel. There were interesting tales of her maternal great-grandparents, Isaac and Isabelle Roskelley, Mayor and Mayoress of Cornwall's capital, Truro, in the early 20th century. One of Isaac's mayoral duties during the war had been to form a battalion when the War Office decided it was short of soldiers in the field. And so, on March 25th 1915, the 10th (Cornish Pioneers) Battalion, the Duke of Cornwall's Light Infantry, was born; commanded by Colonel Dudley Mills, it very appropriately had a crossed pick and rifle on its collar badge.

Stories of another old family member also proved fascinating. A qualified geological engineer, he left his job in Cornwall to work in the gold mines of South Africa;

however, I believe Oonagh's story of him playing cards with Sir Cecil Rhodes, after whom Rhodesia was named, was a fictional one mischievously passed down by her grandparents. Men like this family relative who worked in Cornish tin mines then emigrated to make their fortunes overseas were called Cousin Jacks. There's also an old saying in Cornwall, and no doubt it's true: "wherever you may go in the world, if you see a hole in the ground, you'll find a Cornishman at the bottom of it."

I particularly enjoyed stories of her popular and much-loved paternal grandfather, William Edgar Hawkey. He was a prominent horse breeder who the Government employed to procure horses

Cornish mine sketch taken from an old Hawkey family sketch book

Wiliam Edgar Hawkey

for use in World War 1 and due to his equine experience, his services were always in great demand at West Country agriculture exhibitions. Like many West countrymen, he loved rugby, was a member of the County's Selection Committee and spent many years as Chairman of Falmouth Rugby Club. His other love was that ancient martial art sport, Cornish wrestling, and he often acted as a stickler (referee) in their matches. He had two children, a son and a daughter. Sadly, he lost his son, Edgar, in World War II and his daughter Gwendoline when she was only 22 years old.

After William died, his wife, a generous, kind, indomitable lady whom I knew as Grannie Hawkey, stayed on in their beautiful house, Trescobeas Manor in Falmouth. I remember visiting her there with my mother and being very impressed with her beautiful home, set in extensive grounds. A few years ago, feeling nostalgic, I went back to find the manor, only to discover it had been demolished.

On April 25th 1953, Grannie Hawkey gave 6 acres of her Trescobeas' land to Falmouth Cricket Club and requested they name their new home in memory of her late husband. The club needed somewhere to play as they had been using the Falmouth Recreation Ground for their games; however as that was used all winter for rugby, the cricketers struggled to get a good wicket on it at the beginning of the summer so a ground of their own was sorely needed. The

inauguration of the club's new land was

included in the town's Festival of Britain festivities, and the following statement came from the Club's Chairman, Mr R Fiddick. He said, "When this cricket club is finished, we shall have something of which Falmouth can be proud."

In April of this year, they will celebrate 70 years of playing at Trescobeas, and I know from recently speaking to the Club's Chairman, that Grannie Hawkey's generosity has never been forgotten.

William's son Edgar married Marjorie May, Oonagh's mother, in the 1930s, and at that time, theirs was only the second fencer's wedding to have taken place in Falmouth. As the happy couple came out of the church, it must have been an impressive sight as they passed under an arch of foils formed by a guard of honour. Edgar and Marjorie were both very active in Falmouth sporting circles and were also prominent members of the Falmouth Little Theatre Players, so it was somehow fitting the bride should walk down the aisle to the wedding march from the show "Lilac Time."

Oonagh was incredibly proud of her father, Edgar, an RAF Coastal Command gunner,

Aunt Oonagh's parents wedding- late 1920's – Falmouth

Aunt Oonagh with her father Edgar Barry Hawkey who died as a result of being wounded in WWII

Air gunner badge of Edgar Barry Hawkey

Alan and Oonagh's wedding - St. John's Church Locksheath

whom she loved very much but sadly didn't have in her life for very long. Wounded during a dangerous mission in World War II and risking his own life to save a colleague, he tragically died in 1944 from his injuries when he was only 35.

Alan and Oonagh eventually chose a date for their wedding after his ship returned to Portsmouth. My grandmother, Violet, was kept very busy working on her trusty Singer sewing machine; being a treadle-type one, it made a lot of noise as she treadled away, making outfits for herself, the bride, the bridesmaids and the groomsboy.

The happy pair were married on August 1st 1953, in St John's Church, Locksheath, and it seemed the whole village turned out to wish them luck. Alan looked smart in his Royal Navy uniform, and the bride was a

Joan, Barbara and Mary. Bridesmaids at Aunt Oonagh's wedding 1953

picture in her beautiful cream silk dress. My mother, her Maid of Honour, looked stunning in cerise satin, while Mary, Oonagh's stepsister, and I looked demure in white chiffon. Completing the tableau was her much-loved stepbrother Arthur, charm personified, in his groomsboy outfit. The newly married couple were bombarded with confetti as they left the church, and the village children rushed over to give them lucky silver paper horseshoes on ribbons. If memory serves me right, the Locksheath chimney sweep, suitably attired, covered in soot, and ready to kiss the bride, was waiting outside. They were common sights at weddings when I was young, due to the fact they have always been considered lucky. It started in 1066 when one pulled William the Conqueror out of the path of a runaway carriage and more than 700 years later, another one stopped King George III's barouche from overturning after a dog spooked the horses. Both Kings bestowed luck on all chimney sweeps, and when Prince Philip married our late Queen Elizabeth, it is said one was ushered into Buckingham palace to shake the Prince's hand; however, it's not known if that chimney sweep got to kiss the bride.

It had undoubtedly been a fortuitous meeting for Oonagh and Alan in Sri Lanka. Her much-loved Grannie Hawkey and Grannie May, both from Cornwall, were honoured guests at her wedding, and the newly married couple would go on to enjoy over 50 years of married bliss.

In 1960, seven years after the wedding, Alan was selected to serve on HMS Dreadnought. It was a proud moment for him and the rest of the crew when, on October 21st 1960, at Barrow-in-Furness, Britain's first nuclear submarine was launched by Her late Majesty Queen Elizabeth II.

Alan followed his years on the atomic submarine with postings as an instructor at naval establishments in various parts of the British Isles: at Dounreay in the Highlands of Scotland and at HMS Sultan in the Hampshire town of Gosport. His last few years, which I know were happy ones for him, were spent on the County-class destroyer HMS Glamorgan. Finally, as a fitting end to a successful career, he was employed as a senior-technical author for the Ministry of Defence, spending much of his time travelling backwards and forwards to shipyards in Belfast.

My Uncle was always very guarded about his work but after retiring he would often regale us with tales of what life had been like under the sea for months at a time in a nuclear submarine during the years of the Cold War. I loved listening to his stories as his maritime adventures all sounded very dangerous and exciting.

Chapter 5

Sometime in the 1930s, the Potters moved to a terraced house in Titchfield Common and became active members of Locksheath Congregational Church. In the early days of the 20th century, garden parties and fetes were a popular way of raising money to pay for the maintenance of church buildings and for supporting missionaries overseas. Although they may not sound exciting now, in those early days, church village affairs were often the highlight of the year. The ones my grandmother and her friends organised included thrilling competitions such as "Guess the weight of the cake" and "Guess the dolly's name," and there were also raffles, tombolas and various games for the children.

Violet was eventually appointed Treasurer of Locksheath Church's Sisterhood, a

Violet's Locksheath Sisterhood Badge

Joan with her mother and grandmother

ladies-only club founded by the Reverend Boxall's wife in 1927. Her close friend, Mrs Tutton, affectionately known to me as Aunty Topsy, served as President. A guest speaker was invited each week to talk to the ladies, and I remember one coming to lecture on the subject of Polypodiopsida from the Antipodes. She managed to lose her audience completely when she bombarded them with the complicated Latin names of her subject: ferns from Australia. Suddenly, her projector misbehaved and spewed hundreds of transparencies over the floor. The ladies could hardly conceal their mirth as the poor speaker, quite disconcerted, gathered up her slides with the President's help and

replaced them in her projector. To her credit she then gamely carried on as if nothing had happened.

Sisterhood meetings always began with the Sankey hymn, "Let the beauty of Jesus be seen in me." The pianist was a charismatic lady, known to me as Aunty Maud, who thumped the piano enthusiastically, if not always accurately; sometimes, we struggled to catch up with the music, and sometimes, all seemed to be singing a long way behind it. Ladies of the Catering committee delivered almost undrinkable tea in a large urn which they dragged across the floor on an antiquated trolley. As they manoeuvred it up and down the narrow aisles, it rattled noisily, disrupting the afternoon's proceedings. When attending the meetings, I was often asked to sing and the most frequent request was the Rev. George Bernard's "The Old Rugged Cross." This very emotional hymn with inspirational words invariably moved many of the ladies to tears.

My grandparent's house was in the middle of a terrace of three. Two elderly spinster ladies lived next door on the right, and a charming but somewhat reclusive widow with a yappy but adorable Pekinese dog lived on the left. The elderly ladies spent their days making creamy pink and white coconut ice bars which they generously distributed to the village children. As pocket money from parents was either very little in those days or, in most cases, non-existent, we all appreciated this heavenly confectionery that came our way. The house had a typical English country garden with beds of roses bordering uneven lawns in the front, and an overgrown red and white fuschia partially blocking the sitting room window. There was an Anderson shelter at the back, with red-and-black-currant bushes on one side and a vegetable patch on the other. A beautiful lilac tree had grown close to the kitchen window, but

sadly, I was never allowed to pick its'
pretty flowers. Tradition held it was popular, along with the hawthorn, with those wild, unpredictable creatures called faeries and, as people were somewhat superstitious in those days, it was deemed sensible not to display their blooms in your home.

The property directly opposite the Potter house was a smallholding belonging to a couple called Nelly and Harold, who lived there in perfect harmony with Nelly's brother, Walt. Harold loved to spend his days lounging against his five-bar gate, chewing a piece of corn and watching the world go by; however, he always had a ready smile and time for a quick chat with anyone walking past. I was often sent to buy their new-laid eggs, which were always a delicious breakfast treat for me; their rich yellow yolks running enticingly over toast soldiers dripping with butter.

As well as organising fetes and bring-and-buy sales to raise money for the church, Violet ran progressive whist drives for the NSPCC (National Society for the Prevention of Cruelty to Children). I can't remember if these were held weekly or fortnightly, but they were very popular, and the people who played took turns hosting the event in their respective houses. I recall fun-packed afternoons involving lots of badinage and laughter, especially when things didn't go according to plan. Occasionally, one or other of the players would try to progress around the wrong way, or my grandfather, much to my grandmother's dismay, would revoke, upsetting the other players at his table. Tempers occasionally flared, but everything had usually calmed down by the time the tea and cakes arrived.

Locksheath village charabanc outing circa 1947

My mother attended the St John the Baptist Church of England School and although she was not of a scholarly disposition, she was nevertheless bright. Her favourite subjects were English language and literature; she especially enjoyed plays, and acting would become one of her hobbies later in life. Her love of theatre came from her father, a natural-born extrovert who loved being on the stage. I remember when I was taken to see him in the pantomime Aladdin at Sarisbury Green Community Centre in the late 40s or early 50s. I vividly remember screaming with fear when he was put through the mangle by Widow Twankey in the laundry scene and came out the other side as a cardboard cut-out. I was convinced I would never see my much-loved grandfather ever again.

Joan eventually joined the Girl Guides, and although she never mastered any practical skills, she did enjoy the company of the other members. Originally there was a scout movement that was only for boys, but in 1909, at a Boy Scout Rally in Great Britain, a group of girls turned up and proclaimed themselves to be Girl Scouts. Lord Robert Baden-Powell, an army general who founded the male-only movement in 1907, decided to start a similar one for girls, so the Girl Guide movement was born. Their motto, which shares the Founders' initials, is "Be Prepared", and Girl Guiding did then and still does aim to educate their members in good citizenship, good behaviour and the importance of outdoor activities.

Joan chugged along happily with her brother Alan in their early years, although they sometimes fought, as siblings do. However, beneath the surface of childhood antagonism, their deep love and affection

Joan in her Girl Guide Uniform

The Potter family 1943

for each other never wavered throughout their lives.

William and Violet were kind, caring parents to their two children and were deeply loved by them in return. William served in World War II in the RAF but, like most men of his era, never once spoke of his experiences. I remember hearing during the war that he failed to let go of a barrage balloon one day and floated up with it into the sky. My grandmother said he broke a few bones on landing after letting go of the balloon's guide ropes. I was never sure of the veracity of this tale, but as my grandfather was incredibly accident-prone, it could well have been true.

On September 3rd 1939, as World World II began, William and Violet's lives, along with those of Alan and Joan, would change drastically out of all recognition.

Chapter 6

The early months of the conflict were called the" Phoney War" as, although some action was taking place at sea, there was very little military activity on land or in the air. The Allies had stationed their troops along the Maginot line, waiting for the enemy to attack, but despite a few brief skirmishes, no fighting took place. However, it was the lull before the storm as on May10th, the German Army attacked France and the Low Countries. They pushed the Allied troops back toward the coast and trapped them in the port of Dunkirk.

Today, television news programmes provide blanket coverage of fighting taking place in faraway locations, with journalists in safety helmets and combat gear reporting from perilously dangerous front lines;

however, in 1940, things were very different. That year a department called the Ministry of Information was formed to strictly censor all media reporting; this included radio, newspapers and cinema newsreels.

On May 10th 1940, after being attacked from all sides, Neville Chamberlain resigned and Winston Leonard Spencer Churchill became the Prime Minister. The new incumbent immediately formed a wartime coalition government with the Labour, Liberal and Conservative parties, and on May 13th, in a somewhat raspy voice, he addressed the House of Commons and included in his speech the following words:

"I say to the House as I said to ministers who have joined this government, I have nothing to offer but blood, toil, tears, and sweat."

It must have been a truly terrifying experience for the Allied troops trapped in Dunkirk and in danger of being wiped out by the relentless Nazi army. All the escape routes through the English Channel had been cut off, and the soldiers must have despaired of ever seeing their homes and loved ones again. However, the RAF fought hard to protect the stranded men by preventing the Luftwaffe from having complete air supremacy, and the French Army bravely defended the soldiers by stopping seven German divisions from attacking the port. According to military historians their actions in what became known as the Siege of Lille saved the lives of an estimated 100,000 Allied troops.

On May 26th, Prime Minister Churchill ordered Operation Dynamo into action. As Admiral Bertram Ramsay and his Royal Navy team directed the rescue mission from a network of tunnels deep in the

Dover cliffs, the Prime Minister confided he was only confident of rescuing, at the most, 45,000 men. However, miraculously, by June 4th, 338,226 soldiers had been plucked from the beaches and harbour and returned safely to England. As these men had constituted the bulk of the British Expeditionary Force, it had been imperative for the country's future defence that every last one of them was brought home.

So, on May 30th, a vast armada of small boats, numbering over 850, protected by RAF aircraft, set sail from the port of Ramsgate. It included pleasure craft, fishing boats, cockle ships and vessels of every make and description, including 19 lifeboats. Only two of the latter, one from Margate and the other from Ramsgate, were crewed by RNLI members, and between them, they rescued 3,400 men. Their coxswains, Howard Knight and Edward Parker, each received the DSM

(Distinguished Service Medal) for their heroic efforts.

Although records show naval personnel crewed some of the private boats commandeered by the Admiralty, others were sailed over to France by civilian volunteers. Those private citizens must have had enormous courage to cross the English Channel in their small boats, knowing they were in constant danger of being attacked by enemy aircraft. One such volunteer was a retired Royal Navy Officer, Commander Charles Lightoller, who had been decorated in World War 1 for his bravery under fire. He had experienced a lot of disasters in his life after going to sea at 13. These included being shipwrecked three times, running into an outbreak of smallpox and a revolution after his ship put into Rio de Janeiro during a storm and surviving a life-threatening attack of malaria whilst sailing on the West African coast. He then decided to leave his seafaring days behind him and tried prospecting for gold in the Yukon. That proved unsuccessful, and after a spell as a cowboy in Canada, he eventually worked his way back to England on a cattle ship.

His next employer was the White Star Line, and on April 15th 1912, he was the 2nd Officer on the Titanic, when she struck an iceberg in the North Atlantic Ocean on her maiden voyage to New York. As the ship started to go down, Officer Lightoller leapt into action, ushering as many women and children as possible into lifeboats and helping to launch them into the freezing cold water. At the last minute when the liner was sinking fast, he dived into the sea from the top of the wheelhouse and was sucked into a huge ventilator. Miraculously, a massive blast of hot air from inside the ship propelled him back to the surface. Floundering in the waves, he spotted an upturned emergency collapsible lifeboat nearby, swam in its direction and managed to climb onto it, joining the 30 other survivors clinging to its slippery hull. He helped save their lives by showing them how to shift their weight against the swells to prevent the boat from being swamped.

On hearing Titanic's mayday call, the RMS Carpathia, 58 nautical miles away from the stricken liner and under the command of Captain Rostron, sailed towards her, navigating ice fields on the way. She reached up to 17 knots when her top speed was only 14. Later, when interviewed, the captain was asked how his ship managed to reach the sinking liner so quickly; his reply was, "A hand other than mine was on the wheel that night."

So, it was an experienced mariner, Charles Lightoller, who left Ramsgate on June 1st, two days after the main armada, accompanied by his son Roger and a sea scout called Gerald, to sail to the coast of France. Soon after they left, they were attacked by enemy bombers but luckily the naval destroyer HMS Worcester was nearby. One of her crew members, Harold "Barny" Barnett, is quoted as saying," On one of the return trips, we came across a small boat making its' way back with a load of soldiers; as we came up, it was machine-gunned by German planes, so we joined in with our guns and drove them off. The boat was called Sundowner, owned and skippered by Mr. Charles H. Lightoller, one of the surviving officers from the Titanic."

On approaching the French coast, the Sundowner rescued the crew of a motor cruiser called Westerley, which was on fire. Luckily they had managed to get half a mile away before she blew up with a couple of hundred gallons of petrol on board. On arriving at Dunkirk, the Sundowner came alongside the naval destroyer HMS Worcester, and 130 troops were moved from the large ship onto the small yacht. When the transfer was complete, there were 75 men in Sundowner's cabin and another 55 crammed on her deck. She had only sailed at the most with 21 passengers before, so was dangerously overloaded when she set off to return to Ramsgate. The boat was attacked several times on their way back, and at one time, just as an enemy fighter plane was bringing her guns to bear, Commander Lightoller managed to evade them with a trick learnt from his son, an RAF pilot. When the Sundowner arrived back at Ramsgate and 130 men disembarked from her, the Chief Petty Officer, counting the returned soldiers, remarked," My God, mate, where did you put them all?

Another person of note who took part in the Dunkirk evacuation was First Lieutenant

F.G Woods, an HMS Worcester crew member. He previously served on HMS Thetis and was one of only three people to survive the British Navy's worst submarine disaster when she sank during sea trials in Liverpool Bay in 1939. Lt. Woods was later awarded the DSO (Distinguished Service Order) for his work during the Dunkirk evacuation and for bringing his ship's gunnery up to such a high standard after her recommission.

The following story from a soldier named Gunner Kester illustrates the vital role of the Royal Navy in the evacuation. He and his comrades were on the beach at La Panne in the early morning hours, waiting to be picked up, and, according to him, only got lucky when HMS Worcester appeared. They sailed out to her in small boats and, to board her, had to climb up her side on rope ladders. Gunner Kester was finding it hard going as he'd been wounded in his shoulder when suddenly there was a shout from above telling him, with typical British humour, he was holding up the cinema queue. On realising the gunner had a problem the crewman leant over, grabbed his webbing braces and hauled him bodily onto the deck. Gunner Kester said when they entered Dover at 07.30 on May 31st, all the destroyers sounded their sirens, and for the rest of his life, that noise, whenever he heard it, would send shivers down his spine. Making his way off the ship, the gunner looked around for his "sailor buddy" who'd pulled him on board but couldn't see him or any of the ship's company, so, instead, he thanked the destroyer for bringing him home. The next day it was sad news for him to hear that HMS Worcester was dive-bombed on another rescue mission, with the crew suffering many casualties. Almost two years later, when reading of the infamous Channel Dash, the gunner said he felt great pride in learning the vessel that had rescued him and his fellow soldiers from the beaches of Dunkirk had also played such a brave part in that seagoing action.

Merchant ships of Great Britain were also heavily involved in the rescue mission, none more so than the S.S. Clan MacAlister, a cargo vessel from Glasgow. She was in Southampton when the Admiralty requisitioned her, and after she had been loaded with eight landing craft, she sailed for Dunkirk. Although two of the craft were damaged when being unloaded, the other six began evacuating the troops. Later, the ship was bombed, killing 18 of her crew, and the surviving members were rescued by two naval vessels.

The whole country applauded the heroes who had brought the soldiers home from Dunkirk in circumstances of great danger, and many were honoured for their heroism.

Charles Lightoller received a Mention in Despatches for his part in the operation.

Prime Minister Churchill said," the whole root and core and brain of the British army" had been stranded at Dunkirk, and he told the people of Britain their return had been a "miracle of delivery."

Speaking to the nation on June 4th, it was reported he was trying to raise the low morale in Britain and also appeal for support from America, as he included the following words in his speech in the House of Commons:

"We shall go on to the end, we shall fight in France, we shall fight on the seas and oceans, we shall fight with growing confidence and growing strength in the air, we shall defend our Island, whatever the cost may be, we shall fight on the beaches, we shall fight on the landing grounds, we shall fight in the fields and in the streets, we shall fight in the hills; we shall never surrender.

Chapter 7

I found a photo of my Uncle with HMS Worcester's officers at Poplar dockyard when the ship was taken in for repair after Dunkirk. Although he'd never spoken of the evacuation, I thought this photo might suggest he'd been involved in it, but I was wrong. According to naval records, Gunner Wellman joined the ship in August 1940. However, he was serving on her in 1942 when she was involved in the Channel Dash, referred to by Gunner Kester in the previous chapter. The action occurred when the German pocket battle cruisers Scharnhorst, Gneisenau and the heavy cruiser Prinz Eugen sailed through the Dover Straits, trying to escape from the French port of Brest. A combined Naval and Airforce operation took place in an attempt to destroy or disable the ships, but the

This photograph of the new CO, "Dreamy" Coats, and his officers was taken in Poplar Dock, East London, while she was undergoing repairs after Dunkirk
Back row left to right: Sub. Lt. Dennis Williams RNVR, Sub.Lt. Ronald Hardman RNR, C.Eng. Hugh Griffiths RN, Lt. F.W.L. Winterbottom RN, **Gunner (T) L.G. Wellman**
Seated left to right: Lt. F.G. Woods RN , Lt.Cdr. E.C. Coats RN, Lt. Morgan RNVR
Two officers killed at Dunkirk are missing: Sub Lt Humpreys joined on the 20 April and died from his wounds on 2 June 1940 and 26 year old Wt Engineer Thomas Smillie from Dumbarton who served in several V & W destroyers
Courtesy of Vic Green

mission failed, and many lives were lost. HMS Worcester was one of the vessels in the flotilla and she was hit by shells from all three German ships. In the silence that followed the bombardment, a member of her crew Sub Lt. Bill Wedge, looked around and, seeing no movement, thought no one could be alive, especially after the battering the ship had taken. Then he saw Gunner Wellman lying on the deck, injured but still conscious. He thought they were the only officers who had survived so he was greatly relieved when their Number one, Lt. Anthony Taudevin, appeared. Those that were not too badly hurt made superhuman efforts to save their wounded colleagues but, sadly, 27 crew members died in this action..

The three battleships eventually arrived back in Wilhelmshaven in Northern Germany, to Hitler's relief and the Allies' despair. Many commendations were awarded for bravery during this operation, and my Uncle, Gunner Wellman, received a Mention in Despatches. Although we knew he had received this commendation for his courageous actions, he never once spoke of his experiences during that fateful "Channel Dash." Later in his career, he was promoted to the rank of Lieutenant Commander and served on a naval base in Malta and one in Norfolk, where, with my mother, I have fond memories of visiting him.

Leonard George Cornish Wellman, my Uncle Bill, was a tall, handsome sailor from London who, in the late 1920s, swept my grandmother's sister, Doris, off her feet and married her. They adored each other and enthusiastically embarked on naval life, especially enjoying the parties where they could socialise with other naval officers and their wives. Both enjoyed a drink, and I remember they always carried a custom-made wooden case containing all the accoutrements with which to mix their beloved gin and tonics.

When Uncle Bill eventually retired, he became the landlord of a pub called the Fort Wallington Tavern in Fareham, a drinking establishment very popular with naval personnel from HMS Collingwood and HMS Sultan. He and Aunty Di had no children, so enjoyed having me stay with them. I loved the pub's atmosphere, and if the sailor's darts teams were a member short, they would, to my delight, ask me to play with them. The lifestyle was very unhealthy as it was at least 1.30 am by the time we had cleaned up the bar, and dinner, which appeared around 2 am, usually consisted of sausage and chips cooked in a deep-fat fryer.

I remember going through a stage of wanting to appear sophisticated when I visited them and asking if I could have an alcoholic drink, but they said, at 14, I was far too young. However, after I continued to pester them, they gave in and decided to teach me a lesson by pouring me a long peddlar. As this drink consists of a fairly large slug of sloe gin, it knocked me for six, and I remember sliding down the wall only to come to when their German shepherd guard dog started licking my face with great enthusiasm. It was a long time before I ever asked for another drink containing alcohol.

Chapter 8

The Government made the decision to evacuate children from cities and towns expected to be targeted by bombers. Seeing the little ones clutching their small suitcases and junior gas masks, with name labels around their necks, must have been a heartrending sight. How hard it must have been for them all as they clung to their parents, waiting for trains to take them away to God knows where.

In January 1940, basic foods such as butter, bacon, and sugar were rationed; however, vegetables and fruit were exempt even though things like onions and tomatoes, shipped from overseas, were often in short supply. The Government encouraged everyone to grow their own produce in gardens or allotments, and "Dig for Victory" became a famous slogan.

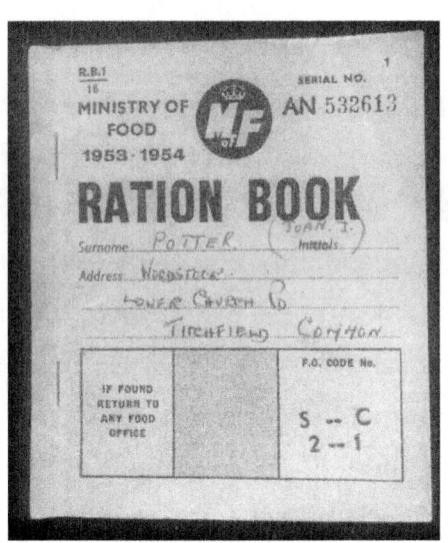

Joan's Ration Book

National Id Card

Wickham Agricultural Committee. *By kind permission of the Hampshire Post*

Land Army Badge

85

In this book's illustrations there is a photo reproduced by kind permission of the Hampshire Post, which may be of the local Wickham Agriculture War Committee. Their purpose was to advise local farmers and market gardeners on how to increase agricultural production. My grandfather, Millard, sat farthest left in the photo, was on this committee, and he and the other members worked tirelessly to help those growing crops to achieve their highest possible yields. During those turbulent years when Britain was at war, the ceaseless toil of farmers, market gardeners, and families growing their own fruit and vegetables was invaluable in helping to feed the country's population.

Many ladies became Land Girls during the war, and while the male agricultural workers were fighting overseas, they played a crucial role in growing food to feed everyone. In those less enlightened times, there was some scepticism about a woman's ability to do a man's job but the Land Girls confounded the critics, as did those working in ammunition and other factories; they all proved they were well up to doing the same work as the men and doing it equally as efficiently.

Although many things were rationed, almost every town and village had its "spivs". These were often petty criminals who traded in black market goods and, for the right price, could get anything you wanted from a fillet steak, a pound of sausages, a bottle of whisky or even a new pair of nylons.

On May 14th 1940, Sir Anthony Eden, the Secretary of State for War, formed the Local Defence Force, a body of men to protect the country from potential invaders. A call had gone out for volunteers, and the

1.5 million people who applied would, as the war progressed, play an essential role in Britain's defence. They wore LDV armbands until issued with proper uniforms and carried any old weapons they could lay their hands on. These included World War I bayonets on poles, rifles, double-barrelled shotguns, pickaxes and all manner of farming implements. Most members had to rely on their own vehicles for transport, although a few platoons were issued with armoured cars. The BBC programme "Dad's Army," set in the fictional town of Walmington-on-Sea, led by the somewhat pompous but endearingly patriotic Captain Mainwaring, faithfully recreated these military volunteers who became known as the Home Guard. In addition to that fine body of men, sterling work was done by all the Civil Defence Volunteers who helped keep Britain safe: among them, the ARP (Air raid precaution) Wardens, firewatchers, first-aid workers and messengers. Also playing its part in World War II was the WVS (now the WRVS), Woman's Royal Voluntary Service, founded by Stella Isaacs, Marchioness of Reading, in 1938. Their members organised, among other things, the billeting for evacuated children and the clothing collection for those in need. When the troops returned from Dunkirk, they were there to give them much-needed hot drinks, sandwiches, warm coats, and jumpers. They were also invaluable during the Blitz, and while the firefighters fought fires, these indomitable ladies, despite the danger, supplied them with endless cups of tea.

Chapter 9

News came of Paris falling to German forces on June 14th 1940, and France capitulating 8 days later. It was a frightening time for all of Europe, and I'm sure my father, full of youthful enthusiasm, could hardly wait to be called up. However, because he was only 14, he would have to wait three more years, as when the National Service Act came into force on May 3rd 1939, only men between 18 and 41 were subject to conscription.

To Hitler's surprise, Britain decided to fight on after the fall of France. There was to be no peace settlement as he'd expected, so he ordered his Army to prepare for Operation Sealion, an amphibious and airborne assault on the country. German forces had already occupied the Channel Islands, and the people of Great Britain were fearful the enemy soldiers would also invade their sceptred isle and impose Nazi rule on them too. Hitler knew that if such an attack were to be successful, air superiority would be crucial, so Reichsmarshall Goering was instructed to send in the Luftwaffe to pave the way. On July 10th 1940, German planes began a three-and-a-half-month-long series of bombing raids, initially targeting channel shipping, ports, radar stations and RAF airfields. Later, industrial powerhouses, communication centres and coastal command stations also came under attack.

Hitler had initially ordered bombs to be dropped only on military targets outside of London; however, during one nighttime raid on August 24, a group of German planes drifted off course and accidentally targeted the City, causing civilian deaths and considerable damage. The Prime Minister retaliated by immediately ordering the bombing of Berlin, and Hitler, in a counter retaliation then ordered sustained bombing attacks on London and other large towns and cities.

The part of the Battle of Britain known as the Blitz began on Black Saturday, September 7th, when the Luftwaffe bombed the capital for 57 consecutive nights. Later, there would be nighttime attacks on harbour installations at Liverpool, Glasgow, Bristol, and other industrial centres like Coventry and Birmingham. On September 15, in a last-ditch effort by the Luftwaffe to destroy Fighter Command, London was subjected to an intensely concentrated daytime attack. The RAF pilots bravely and successfully fought off the enemy aircraft, destroying many in the process. The day this took place is now celebrated as Battle of Britain Day. After this overwhelming defeat, Hitler realised he could not achieve air superiority, so he postponed Operation Sealion and Operation Barbarossa, his proposed invasion of the Soviet Union, became his next objective. Bombing raids and aerial dogfights continued over England into October, although nighttime raids would continue until May 1941. The Battle of Britain officially ended on October 31 1940.

The leadership shown by Air Chief Marshal Sir Hugh Dowding of RAF Fighter Command during this time was first-class and crucial to Britain's victory. One of his most important contributions was the Dowding system, the first-ever wide-area ground-controlled interception network involving radar, aircraft, and ground defence. Prime Minister Churchill noted that without it, "all the ascendency of the Hurricanes and Spitfires would have been fruitless", and the system, he said, was "a most elaborate instrument of war, the like of which existed nowhere in the world." On delivering the address at Sir Hugh's funeral, Dennis Healey, the then Secretary of State for Defence, said, "He was one of those great men whom this country miraculously produces in times of peril."

There were almost 3000 fighter pilots involved in the Battle; though mostly British, some were from the Commonwealth, and others from occupied Europe, neutral Ireland and America. They flew their aircraft with consummate skill, all showing incredible courage in the face of great danger. Their success in eventually defeating the enemy was also helped by the RAF's Supermarine Spitfire and Hurricane Hawker planes, considered the best fighter planes in the world. Sadly, the aeronautical engineer who designed the Spitfire, R.J. Mitchell died in 1937, not knowing his iconic aircraft had made such a magnificent contribution in helping to save his country.

The work of the 30,000 primarily civilian volunteer members of the Observer Corps who scanned the skies from 1000 observation posts checking for incoming enemy aircraft proved invaluable, as did the members of the WAAF (Women's Auxiliary Air Force). Those brave and dedicated women also played significant roles in the Battle, working as plotters in the Sector Station Operations Rooms and helping to maintain and repair the aircraft. In addition, thousands of people worked tirelessly during these critical months to defend Britain, especially the dedicated RAF ground crew, who were tasked to ensure pilots were in their planes, ready to take off and engage the enemy at a moment's notice.

The sustained bombing by the Luftwaffe during this time was unsuccessful in its objective to destroy Fighter Command, and it also failed to demoralise and dishearten the people of Britain. The fearless pilots who fought bravely and selflessly to protect their country were the heroes of the hour. Included in the Prime Minister's impassioned speech in the House of Commons on August 20 1940, were the following words:

"Never in the field of human conflict was so much owed by so many to so few."

It was an apt and fitting tribute to the magnificent airmen who had fought and won the Battle of Britain.

Chapter 10

The Government issued warnings in September 1939 that air attacks on cities were likely, so civil defence preparations began at national and local levels. All families were issued with blackout instructions, to which they mostly adhered. Should even a chink of light be spotted in someone's window, the air raid wardens who patrolled the streets at night would alert the householders to the danger they were causing and, if necessary, issue them with heavy fines. In London, despite a government ban, people still flocked to the underground when the sirens sounded or made for the specially constructed public air raid shelters.

At 6 pm on September 3rd, a few days before the Blitz began, King George VI broadcast to the nation, and those who listened to him all over the country were greatly encouraged by his words. The King held the rank of Admiral of the Fleet and Field Marshall of the Royal Air Force, and he endeared himself to his troops with his eagerness to visit them close to the battlefield's front lines. He also understood what they were going through, having seen action himself during World War 1 in May 1916 while serving as a Turret Officer on HMS Collingwood during the Battle of Jutland. The King is the only British Sovereign to have seen action in battle since William IV in the 18th century. After he qualified as an RAF pilot on July 31st 1919, and was promoted to Squadron Leader, King George VI would also become the first British King to qualify as a pilot. Sadly, later in his life, in 1942, his younger brother, Prince George, the Duke of Kent, was killed in a military air crash, a sad loss that would give him a feeling of empathy with his subjects, who, as the war progressed, were also losing their loved ones.

It was said that the royal family were unsure at first of Winston Churchill when he became Prime Minister; however, over the years, as Britain fought for its very survival, the King and the Prime Minister developed a strong friendship and a bond of mutual respect.

Queen Elizabeth played her part in helping the war effort in many ways. One of them was to commission a fundraising book in 1939 containing 50 contributions from various artists and writers, including T.S. Elliot, Daphne Du Maurier and Ivor Novello. The proceeds went to The International Red Cross, founded in Geneva in 1863. In its own words, the charity ensures "humanitarian protection and assistance for victims of war and other situations of violence."

The people of Great Britain admired the King and Queen for their refusal to leave London when the Blitz began and even more so on Friday, September 13th 1940, when five high-explosive bombs fell on Buckingham Palace. They caused considerable damage, and Queen Elizabeth is quoted as saying, "I am glad we have been bombed. Now we can look the East End in the face." There were concerns for the Royal Family during this dangerous time, and the Foreign Office suggested they should leave the country. However, the Queen stated, "The children will not leave unless I do. I shall not leave unless their father does, and the King will not leave the country under any circumstances whatsoever." The only concession the royal parents made was to send the Princesses

Elizabeth and Margaret to the comparative safety of Windsor Castle.

On October 13th 1940, on Children's Hour, with Princess Margaret by her side, Princess Elizabeth gave her first radio broadcast. She addressed her message to all evacuated children everywhere and told them she and her sister knew what it was like to be separated from those "we love most of all."

Four years later, in 1944, when her sister Princess Margaret became a Girl Guide and Ranger, Princess Elizabeth joined the ATS and qualified as a mechanic and a driver.

The Royal Family was a shining example to the nation during those dark days of conflict.

Chapter 11

When she was 15 and working in Clarks haberdashery shop in Wickham, Joan Potter met Ronald Adams. Although young, Joan was already a beauty. Dark velvety lashes enhanced her dazzling cornflower blue eyes, and her wavy brown hair, tinted with auburn, framed a perfectly shaped face. At their first meeting in Wickham Square, Ronald was immediately captivated by her warm, friendly smile, and after that first meeting, they were inseparable.

They met as often as possible and, both loving nature, enjoyed walking hand in hand along riverbanks and down country lanes. One day, strolling along the path beside the river Meon, they spotted a shy, brightly coloured kingfisher and crept silently toward it, wanting to observe it but determined not to disturb its natural habitat.

Occasionally they would spot a water mole, with its blunt nose and reddish brown fur and laugh as they watched its scaly tail disappear into the reedbeds. When there was no wildlife around, and the water was shallow, they'd kick off their shoes and paddle barefoot through the crystal clear water. The Meon, which flows through Titchfield Haven nature reserve, is a serene and picturesque chalk stream and one of only 300 in the world, most of them being in Southern and Eastern England.

I'm sure Joan and Ronald would have read the story of those amusing characters Ratty, Mole, Badger and Mr Toad in Kenneth Grahame's excellent classic "The Wind in the Willows." And if they had, I'm sure they would have loved it, as it truly captures the magic of river life and true friendship.

Ronald and Joan

On their way home one Sunday, walking past the Sir Joseph Paxton public house, locally known as the Jo, the young couple were surprised to see several middle-aged and elderly men in uniform carrying weapons and marching almost in unison. Ronald immediately recognised them as the Home Guard, the armed citizen militia newly formed to help the Army defend the country in case of invasion.

Like many of their contemporaries, Joan and Ronald's story was one of intense love and devotion, culminating in the inevitable sadness shared by many during World War II. However, for the moment, their romance chugged along happily while the fighting raged on in Europe. They were each other's first and only love, and what began as a simple teenage romance gradually turned into something far more profound; they knew, beyond a shadow of a doubt, they wanted to spend the rest of their lives together.

In 1939, prior to the significant early events of the war, a talented singer called Vera Lynn suddenly burst into the entertainment world. She would become known as the "Forces Sweetheart," bravely travelling as far afield as Egypt, Burma and India to entertain the troops. Her emotional and nostalgic songs boosted their morale and reminded them of their loved ones back home. Joan and Ronald would spend hours locked in each other's arms, dancing to Vera's records in the sitting room, tactfully undisturbed by William and Violet. The two young lovers were trying to savour every moment together as they knew Ronald's inevitable call-up letter would arrive in the not-too-distant future. It's impossible to quantify Dame Vera Lynn's importance to the war effort. Her music would bring desperately needed solace and comfort to the people of Britain during desperate times and her iconic song "We'll meet again" would touch the nation's heart. Parents prayed they would hold their soldier sons and daughters in their arms once more, wives longed to be reunited with husbands, and lovers everywhere hoped against hope that, when their time came to part, they too would one day meet again.

On December 7th, 1941, at 07.55, the Japanese attacked the U.S. naval base at Pearl Harbor. Approximately 20 ships were sunk or damaged, almost 200 U.S. aircraft were destroyed, and 2,403 people were killed. Captain Mitsuo Fuchida sent the following coded message, "Tora, Tora, Tora," to advise his fleet the Americans had been caught by surprise, and by 09.00, the Japanese fleet had withdrawn. Providentially, the U.S. Pacific Fleet's three aircraft carriers escaped being sunk or damaged as, being at sea on manoeuvres, the Japanese could not locate them.

President Franklin D. Roosevelt, the day after the attack, addressed a joint session of Congress and the nation via radio and said, "Yesterday, December 7, 1941—a date which will live in infamy—the United States of America was suddenly and deliberately attacked by the naval and air forces of the Empire of Japan."

By 4 pm, nine hours after Great Britain had declared war on Japan due to their attacks on the British colonies of Malaya, Singapore, and Hong Kong, President Roosevelt had signed the declaration of war on the Japanese Empire. After this atrocious attack on its Naval Base on the Hawaiian island of Oahu, America finally joined the war. They had, however, since September 1940, been helping Great Britain through the Lend-Lease and

Military Aid agreement by providing significant military supplies and other assistance to help Great Britain and Europe in its fight against Nazi Germany.

On 4th-7th June 1942, a crucial four-day sea and air assault, the Battle of Midway, followed the attack on Pearl Harbor. Fortunately, by then, the U.S. Intelligence services had broken the Japanese codes, thus ensuring victory in this battle for the U.S. Pacific fleet.

On January 26th 1942, when the U.S. joined the war, there was an influx of G.I. soldiers into Great Britain. Many of them were generous and showered gifts on the local people. Considering everyone had been starved of luxury for an eternity, this largesse was greatly appreciated; the ladies loved the nylons, the young men the cigarettes, and the Hersey chocolate bars went down a treat with the children. The soldiers also brought jitterbugging over with them, a very energetic form of dancing consisting of somersaults, splits and twirls, which seemed very daring to all the English girls. These young American soldiers would eventually leave for Europe and, not knowing what lay ahead, were determined to enjoy their freedom while they could.

Although it was a heartrending thought, Ronald and Joan knew they would eventually have to part. The young schoolboy from Wickham had been forced to stand by while his country was under attack, and now he was growing older, he was desperate to become a soldier and join in the fight to defend it. I feel sure if he had known of the terrible atrocities being carried out by the Nazi party against the Jewish race and against millions of other people of different ethnicities his determination to fight against such horrific inhumanity would have been even stronger.

Joan supported Ronald wholeheartedly, and whilst she found the thought of him in danger on the battlefield terrifying, she was incredibly proud of his determination to join the fight and help to defend his country.

Chapter 12

The resistance fighters in France played a crucial role in many Allied operations. Their intelligence reports on German troop movements and weapons were invaluable, as were their sabotaging enemy supply and communication lines. They helped Allied soldiers fighting on French soil when under attack and assisted them in escaping if captured. They were all incredibly courageous and risked their lives daily, especially the radio operators who were forced to constantly move due to the danger of being discovered.
.

A secret organisation in England called the Special Operations Executive, created in July 1940, which sometimes worked closely with the French Resistance, was also heavily involved in sabotage and espionage activities. Its members were supplied with false identities and they prayed their cover stories were watertight in the event of being captured. Their lives were constantly in danger when taking part in these undercover operations, and, at the most, they had only a 50% chance of returning from them safely.

Days merged into weeks and weeks into months as the fighting continued. The war was being fought on three fronts: the Russian (or Eastern), the Mediterranean and the African, and suitably censored stories of what was happening on them all would filter through into the British media from time to time.

There would be admiration when people heard of the Dambusters and the remarkable invention of Barnes Wallis. In May 1943, his "bouncing bombs," dropped by RAF's 617 Squadron, successfully destroyed two critically important hydroelectric dams in Germany's Ruhr Valley. In these daring air raids 53 airmen were killed and 3 taken prisoner. The 34 pilots who survived were all decorated for their heroism and Wing Commander Guy Gibson who led the attacks received the Victoria Medal. Sadly, he would later be killed in action in the Netherlands.

After the war, there would be feelings of horror when news filtered through of the millions of Jewish men, women, and children killed in concentration camps and of all the millions of people persecuted and annihilated whom Hitler had deemed to be not fitting the Nazi perception of social norms.

There would also be feelings of sorrow when news of what happened in Leningrad, now St Petersburg, came through. The Russian city was subjected to an 872-day siege in which it's estimated that, under constant bombardment by the German Army, over a million of the city's inhabitants starved to death in the freezing cold.

The Soviet Union, according to historical documents, suffered the highest number of fatalities of any nation during the war; 22-27 million of the country's population died, whilst the figure for the total death count of World War II has been calculated at somewhere between 50-70 million.

The letter Ronald was expecting finally arrived. It had Air Training Corps no 1350 Squadron at the top, with his school's name and address in the top right-hand corner. It was signed by Mr A Palmer, the Squadron's Adjutant and was a general letter to all cadets.
It stated under the National Registration heading:

AIR TRAINING CORPS.

NO. 1350 SQUADRON.

Senior Boys' School,
Harrison Road,
Fareham.

Dear Sir,

NATIONAL REGISTRATION.

I am instructed by the Air Ministry to inform you that you should register under the National Service (Arm Forces) Act on Saturday next the 9-1-43 . I am directed to inform you that you should attend in A.T.C. uniform, and take with you your A.T.C. and National Registration Identity Cards.

In order to make sure that you are duly accepted for service with the R.A.F. or F.A.A. you should attend the Squadron on Monday next the 11-1-43 to notify the Adjutant or Assistant Adjutant of your registration. A return has to be made to the Air Ministry to ensure your admission into the R.A.F. or F.A.A.

I would remind you that you should have Form A.T.C. 2. and if you have not yet applied for this you should do so in person at the next Squadron parade. Without this form you may not be able to obtain admission to the R.A.F. or F.A.A. whichever you choose.

Yours faithfully,

A Palmer

F/O.R.A.F.V.R.
Adjutant, No. 1350 Squadron.
A. T. C.

National Registration Letter

"I am instructed by The Air Ministry to inform you that you should register under the National Service (Arm Forces) Act on Saturday next the 9-1-43"

It advised them to wear their ATC (Air Training Corps) uniforms and bring their Identity cards. Ronald's childhood dream of becoming a soldier was slowly becoming a reality. He attended the registration as ordered and was duly assigned to the Army's First Battalion, the Hampshire Regiment, nicknamed the Hampshire Tigers.

Winston Spencer Churchill was well placed to lead Great Britain in the war, being a direct descendant of John Churchill, 1st Duke of Marlborough. the brilliant General who led England to victory in the War of the Spanish Succession. Winston joined the British Army in 1895, after graduating from Sandhurst Military Academy and saw action in British India and both the Anglo-Sudan and Second Boer War. He proved to be a great wartime prime minister, leading the country with strength and determination, and his superb oratory rallied the people of Great Britain, giving them hope and courage in their darkest hours.

The two Generals, Eisenhower and Montgomery, believed the only way to win the war was by a massive land, sea and air onslaught. Calais was the obvious place to invade, being the closest town to the English coast, and much deception was used to try and persuade the German Army that Calais was indeed the choice.

The City of Portsmouth from where the invasion would be directed, has played an essential role in Great Britain throughout history. The Naval base, established in 1194, was where the warship Mary Rose, the pride of King Henry VIII's fleet, was built between 1509 and 1511. In the face-off between the French and English fleets during the Battle of the Solent in 1545, the King watched from Southsea Castle as she tragically sank, with the loss of almost 600 men. Although the ship's wreck was discovered in 1971 and raised in 1982, it was impossible to recover it completely, and parts remain buried in the seabed. The sections they lifted, now on display in Portsmouth's Historic Dockyard, attract many visitors. Another significant part of British naval heritage also on show is HMS Victory, Lord Nelson's flagship at the Battle of Trafalgar. This 104-gun first-rate ship of the line provides a fascinating glimpse of living conditions at sea in the Georgian era. Navy Day was a tradition which began in the 1920s when Royal Dockyards were open to the public for Navy Week. My mother always took me as I loved looking over the ships. One year we visited my Uncle Alan's submarine, the T-class HMS Trespasser, and marvelled at how he and the rest of the crew could live in such incredibly cramped conditions. My Uncle told me he had to sleep on what looked like a small table; to this day, I never knew whether or not he was joking. On researching my family tree, I discovered that Alan's grandfather, and my great-grandfather, was a Naval Petty Officer 1st Class, born in Kentisbeare in Devon in 1863, who spent most of his life at sea. However, on retiring from the Navy, he was eventually recalled to serve in World War I at HMS Victory's naval base, where he was employed in the Training Centre and when he died his name was etched on the Guildhall Memorial Cenotaph.

In Portsmouth, a bombproof H.Q. was built in December 1942 under Fort Southwick, containing a naval operational centre and a radio station. This labyrinthine network of underground tunnels, home to around 700 people, was initially constructed in 1860 and was where Operation Neptune, the amphibious part of Operation Overlord, under Commander-in-Chief Portsmouth, was planned and organised. Bob Hunt, an expert on the tunnels, tells on his website how his interest in them began when, as a boy, he came across the entrance to one on a family day out. Eventually, on June 6, D-Day, members of the WRNS and other servicewomen would plot the deployment and subsequent return of the invasion fleet from the English to the French coast. A radio station built into the rock face of Paulsgrove chalk pit was vitally important, enabling urgent messages to be sent and received.

The Government had two large air raid shelters built into the chalk pits; one in London Road, the other in Wymering. Mr Frederick Clarke, a Portsmouth-born

**Fred Clarke and his mother who sheltered in Wymering
air raid shelter during World War II**

gentleman, told how he had childhood memories of being driven to Wymering in a Madgwick horse and cart and said as the bombs fell on Portsmouth, he remembers he and the other children slept in 3-tier bunk beds. I found it interesting, despite being very young, that Frederick had memories, albeit fragmented, of his time there, and from our conversations, it was apparent the experience had left a lasting impression on him. The shelter, equipped with first aid facilities and a canteen, was large enough to accommodate 2565 people, although records state that in an emergency, it could take 5000. There were no showers, only lavatories and washrooms, the latter being a godsend to those with babies and toddlers. There were designated smoking areas so parents could go off occasionally for a cigarette or a puff on their pipe, and the shelter even had its own song and dance troupe. A lady called Rosy Layton ran it, and I'm sure she and her fellow artists entertained everyone royally and lifted people's spirits during those frightening times. There are many informative and insightful anecdotes from people who had sheltered in Wymering on Bob Hunt's excellent website <u>portsdown-tunnels.org.uk</u>.

Chapter 13

My father and his school friends would undoubtedly have been astonished had they known the incredible story concerning the Victorian mansion at Bletchley Park in Buckinghamshire, which housed the Government Code and Cypher School. It was there that the Enigma code, the cypher device used by the Nazi military command to encode messages, was cracked.

Knowing the enemy's plans in advance had become a matter of life and death to the Allies in 1941 as U-boats were continually inflicting heavy losses on their shipping in the Atlantic. As more and more ships were attacked, it was feared essential food supplies to the British Isles would be cut off, and desperately needed raw materials and equipment for the war effort, lost.

The codes were believed to be unbreakable, and the Government knew it needed a miracle to crack them, and that is where an exceptionally brainy Cambridge and Princeton-educated cryptographer came in. His name was Alan Turing and he was a brilliant mathematician, computer scientist, logician, and cryptanalyst who, in 1918, when he was only six, had the following comment made about him by his primary schoolteacher: "I have had clever boys and hard-working boys, but Alan is a genius."

Along with this extremely gifted man, it was necessary to find the most highly qualified people to work at this top-secret establishment and for that reason, many academics from Oxford and Cambridge were recruited. Also, a few more staff were taken on after a Fleet St newspaper set a crossword competition where people were challenged to go to the Daily Telegraph's office and complete a crossword in 12 minutes. Quite a few people turned up, and the five that accomplished the task in the allotted time were invited to work at the Park. The same one was published in the paper the following day, and the readers that completed it were also contacted and taken on.

Staff were recruited from the WRNS, ATS, WAAF and the Civil Service, plus a few from America. In 1939 only 200 people were working at the Park, but by the end of 1944, that number had risen to almost 9000. All those employed were obliged to sign the official secrets act and were under strict instructions never to breathe a word about their work, the nature of which would remain secret for many years after the war.

Alan Turing, in Hut 8, worked unceasingly day and night and finally, with a significant contribution from Gordon Welchman, another British mathematician, he invented the Bombe machine; an electromechanical device capable of deciphering the German's encrypted messages to one another.

According to some military historians, cracking the Enigma code for which Alan Turing received the OBE achieved the following: saved millions of lives, helped ensure the population of Britain didn't starve and possibly shortened the war by as much as two years.

It was a miracle the enemy never discovered the existence of Bletchley Park and the Cabinet War Rooms in London; if they had, both locations would, no doubt, have been targeted by bombers and destroyed. The War Rooms were basement offices under the Treasury Building in Whitehall and housed the Wartime Command Centre of the British

Government. After a bomb fell near Downing Street on October 14th 1940, causing damage to No 10 and killing three men on Home Guard duty, it became clear the safety of the Prime Minister and all those working with him could not be guaranteed, so they were relocated to the Cabinet War Rooms. However, there was concern that if the Treasury received a direct hit, those working underneath it would not survive, so the walls and ceilings were quickly reinforced with steel and concrete.

It was in these underground rooms in safe surroundings, that the Prime Minister held his Cabinet meetings and where Chiefs of Staff gathered to discuss strategy and future plans. Everyone had accommodation in the basements, but it's believed although he always took a daytime nap, the Prime Minister only slept in the underground offices for three nights during the war.

A special room disguised as a bathroom was originally a broom cupboard, and from there, the Prime Minister could speak confidentially on a scrambled telephone to President Roosevelt of America. The scrambling equipment to make these crucially important calls possible was far too large to be accommodated in the War Rooms, so they were housed in the basement of Selfridges Department Store on Oxford Street.

After the attack on Pearl Harbor, Prime Minister Churchill, relieved that America had finally joined the Allies, wrote in his History of World War II, "Being saturated and satiated with emotion and sensation, I went to bed and slept the sleep of the saved and thankful."

Chapter 14

My father started his army training in September 1943 at Belsfield, above Lake Windermere, and I have included some excerpts from the letters he wrote to his parents while he was there.

We know Rose and Millard took a holiday at an unknown destination as in one of the letters he writes to say their card has arrived and commiserates with them about the bad weather they're experiencing. "I hope you are having a good time, you better while you've got the chance. Everything is OK here, only it's a bit of a rush. I've loaded dad's old tank pretty heavy for tomorrow - anyway, heavy enough that had to come up a little hill in bottom gear." He tells them potatoes will be a penny a pound from Monday and it will be necessary to drop them to 6s or 5/6 per cwt

Belsfield where Ronald was billeted high above Lake Windemere

Royal Hampshire Regiment – Ronald Adams (top- row 4th from left)

and tells them to send him a wire if that's not satisfactory.

On the 17th, in a letter from Belsfield, he wrote and complained of being tired after having been out all day and follows with, "we threw some grenades first off and then we went over the blitz course we did a lot of crawls and doubling and then force marched back about 4 miles. Our P.T. is getting harder now as we have to do it in boots, but it gives me a good appetite for breakfast." He says, "we all enjoy this training we are like a lot of kids let loose at times. Some have had to go sick and 2 are in Hospital it is quite easy to break your limbs on the obstacles. Yesterday we saw a chap with a broken leg, he did it on one of the things we went over today. There are a good many sprained ankles, legs, and fingers tonight, but they won't report sick until Monday if they do at all. If they do, they can't go out. One fellow is confined to bed he can't walk as he has a bruised heel, all they told him to do was bathe it in hot water." The letter ends, "Well I must close now hoping you are both well. I am Your Loving Son Ron xxx P.S. excuse letter being a little morbid wont you. They never kill anyone"

A week later, he thanked them for the parcel they'd sent and told them, "Well, we went over the blitz course yesterday and what a time we had going over the obstacles and up the river up to our waist in water then 50 yards crawling under barbed wire with a Bren gun firing over our heads. We did that in the morning and had haversack rations only for Dinner, not even a drink. Then they kept us all the afternoon on a mortar lesson and finally doubled us back or rather force-marched. Some of the chaps are pretty stiff after that but for a wonder, I am feeling OK. I had a nasty neck for a couple of days, a blasted wasp stung me right in my 'salt cellar', as you call it. I couldn't get it treated, but it's quite OK now." Ronald mentions he'd heard from his friend Alf who was under driving instruction in Preston, "on carriers or things like a tank but not covered in." His following words are that time is short, and his equipment has been sorted, but there are still a lot of things to do if he wants to miss Jankers. Finishing the letter are the words "Remember me to all the folks, won't you? Thanks for the clothes coupon it came just right. I am really sorry I can't write more often Mum but I have so much to do at night. After I have done this training it should be better. Cheerio for now. I am your Loving Son Ron xxx

The only other letter that survived was dated March 20th 1944 and headed Ward 6 Preston Military Hospital, Fulwood Barracks, Preston, Lancs.

Ronald writes, "Dear Mum and Dad, As you can see by the address, I am in Hospital, I arrived here this morning after going sick. Three of us came here together. One is in bed now with his head hardly visible under bandages" Ronald tells them he has sores on his face and neck, and the doctors don't know what's causing them, and he complains that none of them can go anywhere, not even to the NAAFI. "The food is alright but not enough to keep hunger away so send me something nice as soon as you can will you please. Also, enclose me some cigs and money or I shan't have much to buy cakes and tea in the morning. Someone goes to get us stuff at NAAFI break in the morning, that's when it's time to have a right good feed. We have lovely single beds with two sheets and 3 blankets and a thick bedspread, it will be just like a civvy bed once again. The worst part of this stunt is they won't allow me to wash. They just put one lot of stuff over the other, and it feels pretty dirty." The letter closes with the words," it will be bedtime soon, lights out is at 9, and we are up at 6 am. I don't know how long I'll be here but I hope it's not too long. Cheerio, I am Your Loving Son Ron xxx"

Just 11 weeks after this letter arrived, Rose and Millard's loving son would be preparing to take part in the invasion of Normandy.

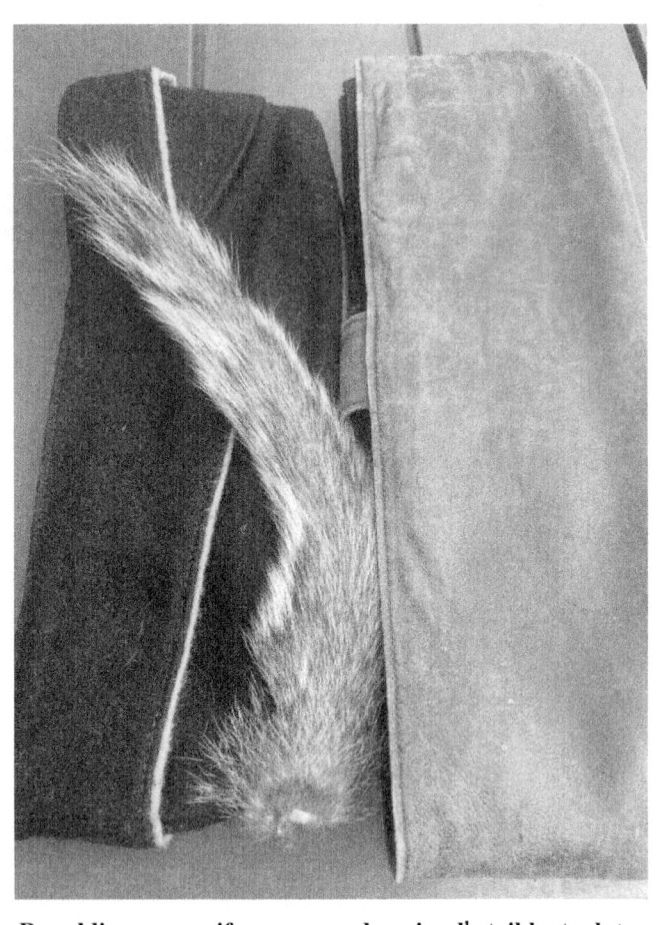

Ronald's army uniform cap and squirrel's tail he took to Normandy for luck

Chapter 15

The young lovers knew they would only have a short time together as rumours suggesting the imminent invasion of Europe were floating around the camp. They believed them to be true and were determined to make the most of every bittersweet moment they had together. Nature, which they had often taken for granted, suddenly became very important to them and they began to find pleasure in many things: sunsets that lit up the skies with flame-coloured hues, droplets of early morning dew looking like small diamonds nestling precariously on iridescent green leaves and stars at night twinkling above them in the sky. The thought of parting filled them both with dread, and that night, the last they would spend together, they lay in a passionate embrace under the trees, clinging to each other as if there was no tomorrow. Ronald cradled Joan's face in his hands, gazing at her with heartbreaking tenderness then gently kissed her eyelids, the tip of her nose and finally, her lips which seemed to melt into his. He tried to drink in her beauty and memorise her face so he would be able to picture it in his mind in the months ahead. He hoped and prayed this would give him the strength to face whatever ordeals he might encounter in the inevitable battles he knew would come.

On discovering his battalion would soon be leaving and knowing there was only a slim chance of him surviving the war, Ronald asked Joan to marry him. His love had grown even deeper over the years, and if, by some miracle, he returned, he knew he wanted to spend the rest of his life with her. He knelt on one knee, produced a small but exquisite three-stone diamond engagement ring from his jacket pocket and gently slid it onto her finger. She was overwhelmed, and her eyes filled with tears of happiness and pain. That moment was the culmination of a love affair that had never wavered for one second and had transported them joyfully through their teenage years despite the war raging around them. That night, under the stars, they made love passionately and intensely, only too aware that the odds were heavily weighed against them ever having a future together. In their hearts, they knew they might never meet again, but, just for that exquisite moment, abandoning themselves to their emotions, they held each other tight, and nothing else in the world mattered.

However, Ronald's belief in his moral obligation to defend his country never wavered for an instant, even though he desperately didn't want to leave the girl he adored. As they said goodbye that night, Joan gave him a photograph to take with him, which she hoped would give him the courage to face the struggles ahead; on the back, she had written the following poem:

God keep and God bless you by night and by day
Fair weather, good fortune and luck all the way
Joan cannot go with you your journey to share
But I'll walk beside you in thought and in prayer.

My father vowed he would carry the photograph with him on his journey into the unknown, and he did.

Chapter 16

In a small village called Droxford, on June 2nd 1944, four days before D-Day, in one of the railway station sidings, top-secret meetings of members of the War Cabinet and some Allied leaders took place. There are various suggestions as to why this particular village was chosen, ranging from its proximity to Southwick House, not being far from the coast, and the tens of thousands of troops stationed nearby. Another suggestion was, as the train would be sitting in a siding close to a cutting with overlying trees, it could be successfully hidden in the event of an attack. There are varying accounts of who was present at the meetings. As well as members of the War Cabinet, the South African leader Jan Smuts, the Canadian President William Lyon McKenzie King, General de Gaulle and President Eisenhower were all reported as being in attendance. An eyewitness remembers seeing Eisenhower, Churchill and possibly de Gaulle in the late afternoon coming out of the tea rooms in Wickham Square. On June 5, with the Prime Minister on board, the train left Droxford station and returned to London, and the following day the Battle for Normandy began.

Lieutenant-General Frederick Morgan and his team of British, Canadian and American officers knew it would be vital for the Allies to secure a bridgehead in Normandy to drive the German Army back from Hitler's Northern European Fortress. So, they drew up a plan codenamed Operation Overlord and after much discussion, the British Prime Minister and the American President chose May 1st for the invasion. However, due to a shortage of landing craft, it was necessary to delay it until the following month. Lessons had been learned from Operation Jubilee, a raid on the Normandy port of Dieppe in August 1942 which went disastrously wrong and resulted in thousands of casualties, mainly among the Canadian forces. The mistakes made in that assault would ensure the D-Day planners covered every eventuality for any future invasion plan.

Prior to these meetings and discussions, in 1942, when ideas for D-Day were embryonic, the BBC devised an ingenious idea. They made a request on-air for postcards and photographs of the coast from Norway to the Pyrenees to help Allied Command find the most suitable sites for the proposed landings. The public enthusiastically responded with millions of postcards and photos finding their way to the War Office; the information they garnered was invaluable. The cards, the visual observations from RAF reconnaissance missions and vital intelligence from the French Resistance played a significant part in helping to decide the most suitable location to launch the most extensive land, sea and air invasion ever attempted in military history.

Any advance warning or even the slightest whisper to the enemy of the chosen destination for the attack would have meant its inevitable failure, so Operation Fortitude South was implemented. It was an impressive plan to tempt the enemy into believing the invasion route would be into Pas de Calais. A fake field army, purportedly commanded by General Patton, constructed of cardboard Sherman tanks, assorted inflatable vehicles and aircraft, was positioned in the South East of England to fool the enemy into thinking the attack would be coming from the Dover area. The ruse worked, and the mocked-up army deceived the usually effective German aerial reconnaissance pilots into believing the massive imitation military build-up they could see from the air was bound for Pas de Calais.

Another factor in hoodwinking the enemy was the arrest of German spies in England who were turned and then forced to feed incorrect information back to their German handlers. One, codenamed Garbo, said to be the most important of the double agents was instrumental in persuading the enemy that Pas de Calais was definitely where the D-Day invasion would take place. King George VI would eventually award him the MBE for his remarkable achievements.

A previous ploy, used earlier in the war, also proved very successful in deceiving the enemy when in July 1943, the Prime Minister and his War Cabinet needed to persuade Hitler they intended to invade Greece and Sardinia and not the island of Sicily. Three British Intelligence officers, Lieutenant Commander Ewan Montague,

Charles Cholmondeley and Ian Fleming, author of the James Bond books, devised an ingenious plan to convince the German high command that Greece was definitely where the allies planned to attack. This ploy involved planting private letters in a briefcase, attaching it to the corpse of a fictitious soldier and then dropping him off the coast of Spain into the sea. It took some time to implement the plan due to MI5's inability to locate a corpse that could pass for someone having drowned. However, eventually, the body of a food poisoning victim was found and deemed suitable, and finally, Major William Martin was born. They dressed the body in the uniform of a royal marine, and then placed personal items in his pockets: family letters, a photo of his fiance, a receipt for an engagement ring, theatre ticket stubs and other pocket detritus. The corpse was then driven to a naval base in Greenock, transferred to HMS Seraph, and safely delivered to Spain.

When the submarine surfaced off the coast of Andalusia, as Major Martin's body was being gently lowered into the water, the Captain read the 39th psalm. A Spanish fisherman found the fictitious marine on the beach at Huelva, a town full of British and German spies. As MI5 had predicted, when the local coroner finally got hold of it, he decided it was indeed that of a man who had drowned. The briefcase, securely attached to the Major's coat, eventually found its way into German hands; they opened it, examined its contents and believed the plans to be genuine. When it was eventually back in British hands, MI5 could tell the Germans had read the letters.

One of them which spelt out plans for an attack on Greece was from Lieut. Gen. Sir Archibald Nye to General Alexander, and another from Lord Louis Mountbatten to Admiral Cunningham. It would have been impossible for M15 to have found more distinguished or highly decorated military personnel than those chosen to be the recipients and senders of the vital letters in Operation Mincemeat. The stature of the men selected undoubtedly added to the letters' authenticity.

Lieutenant-General Sir Archibald Nye, reputed to be Churchill's favourite Deputy Chief of Staff, was wounded twice in action during World War I and was awarded the Military Cross for his "conspicuous gallantry and devotion to duty." In World War II, he proved an excellent Vice-Chief of the Imperial General Staff under Sir Alan Brooke.

Field Marshall The Earl Alexander of Tunis, Harold Alexander, also highly decorated, fought with distinction in World War I and II and assisted in directing the evacuation of the soldiers from Dunkirk in 1940, where records show he was the last man to leave the beaches. Later he formed a successful partnership with General Montgomery when they organised the driving of the German forces back from Egypt and across North Africa.

Admiral Sir John Cunningham, Commander-in-Chief of the Mediterranean fleet during World War II was responsible for the allied landings in the South of France and Anzio. He received many awards for bravery, including the Croix de Guerre, France's military decoration.

Admiral The Earl Mountbatten of Burma, Louis Mountbatten, a great-grandson of Queen Victoria, was highly decorated and served in both world wars. As Supreme Allied Commander South East Asia from 1943 -1946, he oversaw the recapture of Burma from the Japanese and, on September 12th 1945, received their Instrument of Surrender.

On learning from the planted letters that the Allies planned to invade Greece, Hitler removed most of his troops from Sicily, thus paving the way for a successful attack on the island by General Montgomery's British, American and Canadian soldiers. Thanks to MI5's brilliant plan, Operation Mincemeat, Allied casualties in the attack were far less than expected, and their assault on Sicily was successful.

There was previously a cloak of secrecy about whose body was used in the operation. However, as the man's name has now been added to the grave of Major Martin in Huelva, we know it belonged to a Welsh gentleman of the road called Glydwyr Michael. I'm sure Glydwyr would have been delighted to know he had served his country so admirably in the manner of his death.

Chapter 17

The Hampshire village of Southwick, dotted with thatched-roofed and half-timbered cottages, is the setting for Southwick House, originally the ancestral home of the Thistlewayte family. U.S. General Dwight D Eisenhower and the other commanders would follow the invasion's progress on a large plywood map in the operations room. The map spanned from floor to ceiling, and every hour members of the WRNS would climb small ladders and mark on it the positions of the naval forces.

Generals Eisenhower and Montgomery were familiar faces in the unofficial officer's mess, otherwise known as the saloon bar of the Golden Lion pub. Eisenhower developed a taste for whisky during his time at Southwick, so the story goes, but Montgomery drank only soft drinks. A story made the rounds about

Prime Minister Churchill and General Montgomery dining together one night after an inspection of coastal defences. Montgomery told Churchill he didn't drink, didn't smoke, and was 100% fit. Churchill, renowned for his love of brandy, cigars and his rapier-sharp wit, retorted that he smoked and drank and was 200% fit.

Various valuable inventions contributed to the success of the Normandy Invasion. One was Arthur Doodson's tide production machine, which would enable the landings to take place at the safest and most advantageous time due to its ability to predict tidal patterns.

Another was PLUTO, an acronym for the pipeline under the ocean, crucial in transporting the necessary fuel supplies from Britain to Europe for troops and vehicles landing after the invasion.

The most ingenious invention without which the invasion could never have taken place was the mulberry harbours. These were transported in sections to Normandy after June 6th, and were assembled on arrival, thus enabling the rest of the Army, its vehicles and supplies to land in France after D-Day.

Something else that also played a crucial part, not just on D-Day but also throughout the Battle of Normandy, was the Hobart's Funnies. These were the brainchild of Major-General Sir Percy Hobart and were modified tanks that he designed without which, many historians believe, the invasion could not have been successful.

On May 31st, the 1st Hampshire regiment piled into their army vehicles and left their camp in the New Forest, bound for Southampton. The soldiers must have had conflicting emotions as they sped away from the picturesque village of Beaulieu. There was, I'm sure, a mixture of excitement, fear and trepidation, and deep sadness at leaving their families and friends.

On arrival at the port, they poured out of their open-topped army trucks and, weighed down by their equipment, scrambled up the gangways onto the decks of the infantry landing ships docked in Southampton Harbour. It would be five days before the Empires Spearhead, Crossbow, and Arquebus sailed them across the channel. Although I'm not sure which ship my father sailed on, I do know the Brigade Commander visited the troops and wished them Godspeed the day before their departure.

.

Prior to the invasion, in the early hours of June 6, after pathfinders had flown into Normandy to mark the drop zones, approximately 18000 paratroopers from U.S., Canadian, and British divisions were dropped onto the Cotentin peninsula. Their aim was to capture crucial sites behind the invasion beaches and secure the surrounding areas. Due to bad weather, darkness and enemy gunfire, the pilots could not drop the paratroops as precisely as planned, and as they landed, they were scattered in all directions.

A few of the U.S. 82nd Airborne division, after jumping out of their plane, found themselves floating toward Sainte-Mère-Eglise's Town Square. They were an easy target for enemy fire due to light coming from a burning house, and many were shot and killed. One man, Private John Marvin Steel, was saved when his parachute got caught on the church steeple and, knowing German soldiers were close by, he hung motionless for 2 hours, pretending to be dead. He was eventually taken prisoner but escaped and successfully rejoined his regiment. By 04.30, they had captured the town. Many other paratroopers who had been dispersed all over the place eventually managed to link up with each other and went on to achieve most of their objectives. They secured vital approaches to the Allied beachheads and destroyed many German strongholds. Men from the British 6th Airborne Division accomplished their tasks, including destroying the bridges on the Dives river.

After the war ended, Private Steel became an honorary citizen of Sainte-Mère- Eglise, and to this day, an effigy of him hangs from the church tower. Also, inside the town's Notre-Dame-de-l'Assomption Church, there are two beautiful stained glass windows in memory of the 12 paratroopers killed while liberating the town.

The Allies needed to capture two strategically important bridges: one over the Caen Canal and the other over the River Orne. The operation to take and hold them was carried out by men from D company of the 2nd battalion of the Oxford and Buckingham Light Infantry (part of 6th Airborne Division) under the command of Major John Howard. They took off from RAF Tarrant Rushton at 00.16 on June 5th and were transported in 6 gliders towed by Halifax bombers to their objectives. The bridges were taken within half an hour after a brief exchange of fire. The mission was successful due to the element of surprise, although, sadly, there were casualties. Among them was Lance-Corporal Fred Greenhalgh, who was knocked unconscious during the landing and drowned after being thrown from his glider, and Lieutenant Den Brotheridge, who was the first casualty of D-Day when he was shot and killed. He received a posthumous Mention in Despatches for his bravery.

Later in 1944, the Benouville bridge would be renamed Pegasus in honour of the 6th Airborne division, whose uniform emblem was the winged horse of Greek mythology. After the war, the bridge at Ranville would be known as Horsa bridge; Horsa being the name of the gliders who flew in the soldiers to capture the bridge.

Chapter 18

In the days leading up to the invasion, General Rommel inspected the coastal area around the Atlantic wall and, deciding there were insufficient obstacles on the beach to hold back a sea invasion, ordered his soldiers to work round the clock to put many more in place.

Group Captain James Stagg, the chief meteorological adviser, recommended to General Eisenhower that he should not go ahead with the planned invasion on June 5 due to data showing a storm was predicted for that day. He told the General he was convinced there would be a break in the weather on the following one. So, 24 hours later than initially planned, on the evening of June 5, ships from 20 different departure points up-anchored and set off for France. They assembled into convoys at a rendezvous point nicknamed Piccadilly

Circus, just off the Isle of Wight. My father would, I'm sure, like many of the other soldiers, have looked back at his homeland as he sailed away and wondered if he would ever see it again. The following morning he would be part of over 156,000 American, British and Canadian forces to land on the fiercely defended beaches of Normandy. According to naval records, although issued with pills to prevent it, many men were seasick. They must all have had a stomach-churning fear of what lay ahead on their journey across the channel.

The invasion beaches had all been divided into five sections: Omaha, Utah, Juno, Gold and Sword. Ronald's battalion, the Hampshires, was to go in on the right of one part of Gold beach, whilst the 1st Dorsets and 2nd Devons were to go in on the left. At 05.30, the naval bombardment of Gold began, and at 07.25, the landing craft were launched into a high north westerly wind, making navigation difficult. They beached approximately 30 yards from the sea's edge, and as the soldiers jumped into the water, they immediately came under small arms fire. It must have taken all their reserves of courage to reach the sand dunes as, dodging the gunfire, they waded through the dangerous objects hidden due to the unexpectedly high tide. It was a tribute to the Hampshire Tigers' bravery and combative spirit and the other courageous soldiers of the 50th Infantry Division that, after a day of fierce fighting, the objectives of the day on Gold were achieved; they had secured a beachhead and captured Arromanches.

British soldiers carried out the assault on Sword Beach accompanied by a small group of French soldiers. Their landing craft set off at 07.25 and made safe passage despite the large swell. The first wave of infantry that landed on the eastern side encountered strong resistance, and after being attacked by a German strongpoint, they received many casualties. The 1st Battalion Marine Commando Fusiliers, commonly known as Kieffer's Commandos, were the French soldiers who took part in the invasion. They sailed over on D-Day from a village called Warsash in Hampshire and were among the first soldiers to land. Alongside the British soldiers and the tanks, they fought their way up the beach and went on to liberate the town of Ouistreham. One objective of those landing on Sword, to link up with the Canadian troops from Juno, would not take place until the following morning, and another, to take the City of Caen, would not be realised until July 9th.

The U.S. troops were scheduled to land on Omaha, and their objectives were to secure a beachhead and link up with the soldiers from Utah and Gold. Nothing, however, went as planned. The night before the invasion, the objective of Allied bombers was to destroy the German artillery before the start of the assault, but they missed their targets due to low cloud and poor visibility. The Allied failure left the incoming troops vulnerable, and, at 06.30, they were fired on as soon as the ramps came down on their landing craft. The soldiers suffered horrendous casualties, with some being shot and others drowning. Losing so many of their comrades made it hard for them to clear the heavily defended beach exits. Small groups penetrated the German defences and made improvised attacks, and some of the men managed to scale the high cliffs between the heavily guarded points. They eventually gained two small footholds on the French coast and would go on to achieve their other objectives over the next few days. The soldiers at Omaha had an almost impossible task, and their heroic bravery was awe-inspiring in the face of great danger.

The rugged peninsula at Pointe du Hoc, formally part of the Omaha Beach invasion area, was also the scene of incredibly courageous actions when U.S. Rangers scaled 100ft cliffs using ropes, ladders and grapnels. Their task was to protect the soldiers landing on Omaha and Utah by disabling the artillery battery, which was supposedly high on the cliff. As machine gun fire rained down on them, the soldiers made their way laboriously up the cliffs with some also using grappling hooks fired from their landing craft Assaults. Once they reached the top, they discovered the guns were no longer there and, after searching around, finally located them in an orchard nearby and destroyed them. Many lives were lost in this tragic episode, but the exemplary courage and fortitude shown by the American Rangers is, to this day, the stuff of legend.

There had been a rehearsal for the Utah beach landing in April at a seaside resort in Devon called Slapton Sands, which resulted in the loss of many lives. As the mock invasion took place, German E-boats attacked Allied ships, and it's believed that sadly 749 soldiers were killed.

On Utah, the U.S. troops' objective was to establish a bridgehead at the base of the Cotentin peninsula, which was vital as it would enable the Allies to capture the deep water port of Cherbourg. They landed in four waves at 06.30 in the morning, and the first wave was swept south of their original landing place to a less heavily defended area. The troops on Utah were better situated than those on the other beaches as most of their tanks landed successfully, enabling them to fight off the German forces. Brigadier General Roosevelt's calmness under fire and outstanding leadership were said to be responsible for establishing a beachhead with a relatively low incidence of casualties.

The Canadian troops, plus a small group of British Royal Marine commandos, assaulted Juno Beach. The sea was rough, and casualties were high as their first wave went in and met with heavy resistance from the German troops. However, within two hours of landing, thanks in significant part to the armoured squadrons, most of the coastal defences had been cleared. Once again, the successful outcome on this beach was due to the troops' incredible bravery under fire. By midnight, they had succeeded in some of their objectives, advancing inland and joining up with the British at Sword.

Every soldier taking part in Operation Neptune showed incredible heroism and bravery, and by nightfall, the Allied forces had successfully captured a small area of Nazi-occupied Normandy.

Chapter 19

By midnight almost 25,000 men had landed on Gold beach and had penetrated 6 miles inland, where they successfully linked up with the Canadians from Juno.
The Allies received intelligence from the French Resistance that the German S D. division had pulled out of Bayeux, leaving the way clear for its liberation by the troops of the 50th Northumbrian division. My father and the rest of the soldiers marched resolutely into the town at 9 am on June 7th to an ecstatic welcome.

Opposite Bayeux's Cathedral, there is a plaque attached to a wall which reads: "To the glory of God and in memory of all ranks of the 50th Northumbrian Division who laid down their lives for Justice, Freedom and the Liberation of France in the assault on the beaches of La Rivière, Le

Hamel and Arromanches on June 6, 1944, and in Battle on the field of Normandy. The town of Bayeux, the first town in France to be liberated by the Allied armies, was entered and freed by troops of this division on the morning of June 7 1944."

Bayeux was strategically vital to the Allies and became a transit hub through which thousands of troops and vehicles would eventually pass to combat zones. The streets were too narrow to accommodate their large military vehicles, so engineering units rapidly built a bypass road around it. The town's hospitals were operational and treated both wounded Allied soldiers and civilian refugees. In time, however, the Seminary, now home to the famous Bayeux tapestry, became a temporary working hospital.

On June 3th, Bayeux became the provisional Government seat of the Republic of France until Paris was liberated on August 25th. On June 14th, in Bayeux's Place de Chateau, the leader of the Free French Forces, General Charles de Gaulle, gave his first speech to a very enthusiastic audience.

As well as the town of Bayeux, General Montgomery's plan was for Allied forces to capture the City of Cherbourg at the end of the Cotentin peninsula. This deep water port was strategically essential to enable the Allies to bring in supplies directly from America. The task fell, for the most part, to the U.S. troops from the beaches of Omaha and Utah under the command of Major General J Lawton Collins. The city was bombarded by naval ships on June 25th, and British commandos attacked a southwest suburb of the town to soften the resistance from the German troops. After a month-long, hard-fought campaign, on June 26th, the U.S. soldiers successfully took control of Cherbourg.

In his D-Day plan, General Montgomery had anticipated Caen would be taken very quickly after the troops landed in June; however, when that plan failed, he knew it would be imperative to take Carpiquet airport. That objective fell to the Canadian troops, who endured bitter fighting, especially around the village of Authie, where 37 of their soldiers were brutally murdered. The people of the village, horrified by the massacre of these brave young men who died liberating them, named the corner on which they were murdered the Place des 37 Canadiens in their memory. Other executions of young Canadian soldiers took place at the Abbaye d'Ardenne and Fontenay Le-Pesnel. The S.S. Commander under whose watch a total of 156 Canadian soldiers were murdered, was tried after the war ended and found guilty; however, his original death penalty was commuted to life imprisonment, much to the anger of the Canadian people.

On June 7th, despite the heavy fighting in Authie, the Canadians did not take the village and were forced to retreat to Buron. However, just over a month later, on July 8, after much fierce fighting and many casualties, they finally liberated the village to the great relief of its residents.

During Operation Windsor on 4/5th July, Carpiquet came under Allied control. The Canadian soldiers showed great courage during the ferocious fighting there, and the following day, after repelling several German counter attacks, the village was in their hands. The vitally important Carpiquet airport took several attempts to capture, and it wasn't until nightfall on July 9th that it finally was in Canadian hands.

It was essential to hold Caen as it was a crucial road junction strategically placed astride the Orne river and the Caen Canal; after taking it, the Allies planned to push the German troops back toward Germany. However, on June 19, the Hampshires, having advanced close to the Chateau de Cordillon in an attempt to take the village of Hottot, came under intense shell fire from an elite German Panzer division. My father and, sadly, many other brave men from his regiment were killed in this battle. In a touching gesture of friendship, one of my father's comrades removed the gold signet ring from his finger and returned it to my grandparents after the war had ended.

Ronald Frank Millard Adams was Rose and Millard's only child. He was buried close to where he fell, and a photo of his temporary grave, marked by a simple wooden cross, was sent to his parents by the War Office. They would later advise them that his body would be reinterred in the Cemetery at Bayeux. Sadly, he died not knowing that Joan had conceived on their last night together. I believe, had he known, he would have been glad he had left something of himself to bring love and happiness to both the girl he loved and his parents in the years to come.

Joan was working in Clarke's haberdashery store in Wickham Square when the sad news of Ronald's death was broken to her. She'd known in her heart that he might not return but she was still shocked and grief-stricken after hearing he had been killed in action. Suddenly to the dismay of the other shop assistants who had rushed over to comfort her, she fainted and fell heavily onto the shop floor. Later that day at home, Violet held her daughter in her arms as, totally inconsolable, she sobbed as if her heart would break. My mother never got over losing her handsome soldier, but I knew for the rest of her life, she treasured those joyful years they spent together.

News that Private Adams, Hampshire Regiment, was reported killed in the Normandy on June 19 was received by his parents. As some of his comrades have since been reported prisoners of war, any information concerning him would be gratefully received by Mr and Mrs Adams at their home, Parkside, Blackhill, Wickham.

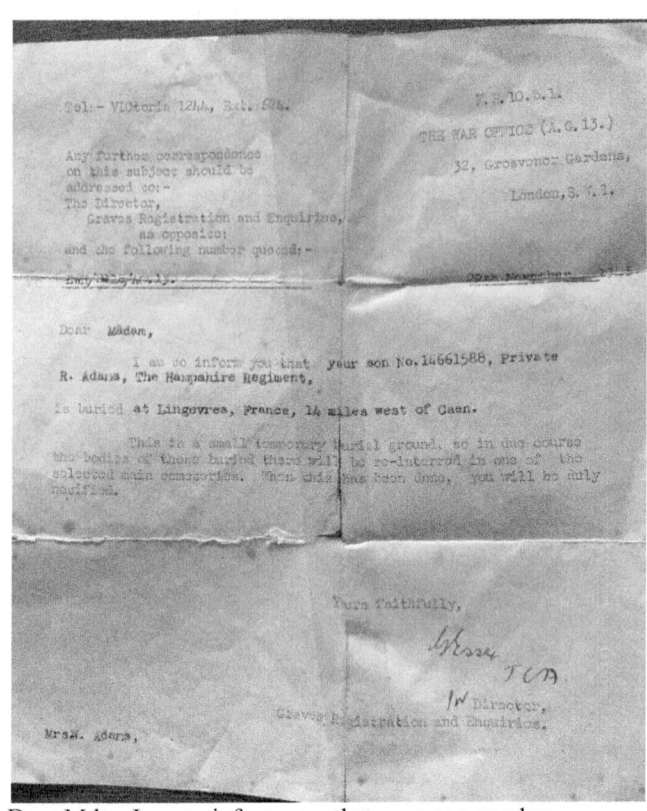

Dear Mdm, I am to inform you that your son number 14661588, Private R Adams, the Hampshire Regiment, is buried at Lingèvres, France, 14 miles west of Caen. This is a small temporary burial ground, so in due course the bodies of those buried there will be reinterred in one of the selected main cemeteries. When this has been done you will be duly notified.

Ronald's temporary grave at Lingèvres

The Under-Secretary of State for War presents his compliments and by Command of the Army Council has the honour to transmit the enclosed Awards granted for service in the war of 1939-45.
The Council share your sorrow that

PTE R. ADAMS

in respect of whose service these Awards are granted did not live to receive them.

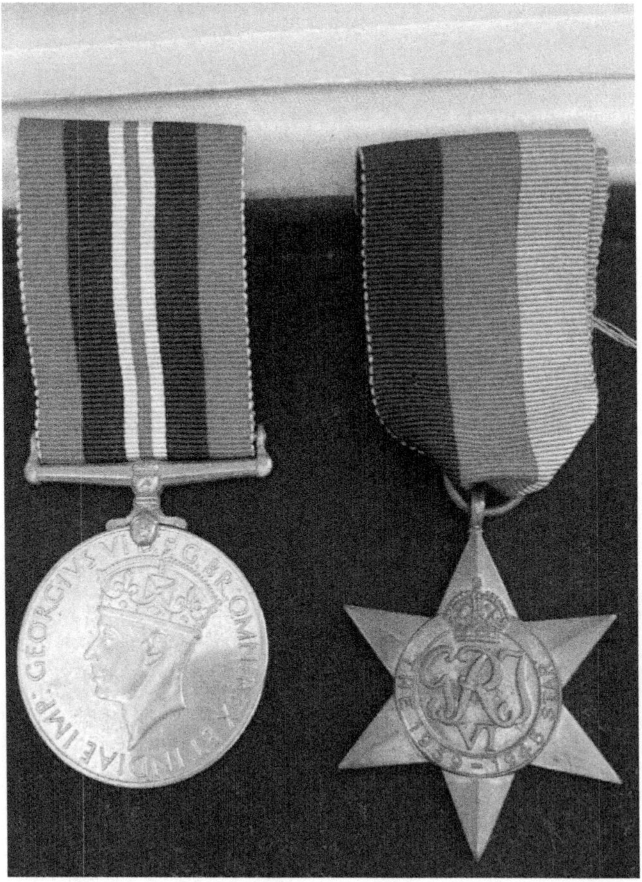

Chapter 20

It would take almost two months of heavy fighting and several military operations before the Allies took Caen, the ancient capital of Normandy. The bombing almost destroyed the beautiful old City, and the casualties among the civilian population and the soldiers on both sides were horrendously high. Because of its strategic importance, capturing Caen was one of the most significant victories of the war and would pave the way for the Allies' advance toward Berlin.

The Battle of the Falaise Pocket, fought on August 12th-21st, followed the capture of Caen, and German forces found themselves almost encircled in an area south of the town of Falaise. They conducted desperate counter attacks to break out to the east over several days, and some escaped; however, military records show that almost 50,000 were taken prisoner. As the German position collapsed in Normandy, Allied forces were free to make their way to Paris.

The military Battle to liberate Paris took place from August 19th 1944, until the German Army surrendered the French capital on August 25th 1944. As General Patton's U.S. Third army approached the City, the French Forces of the Interior rose up against the occupying troops. By August 25th, many other Allied units had also entered the French capital, and the Commander of the German garrison finally surrendered at the Hotel Le Meurice. General Charles de Gaulle arrived and was greeted by Parisians who were delirious with joy at being free at last after four years of oppressive Nazi rule. The General took control of the capital and assumed the mantle of head of the Provisional Government of the French Republic.

After successfully recapturing the French capital, the fighting continued as the Allies pressed on toward Germany. As winter approached, on December 16th, Hitler launched one last offensive in the Ardennes Forest. Churchill would call the fighting that followed "the greatest American battle of the war". It was brutal, fought in freezing conditions, resulted in exceptionally high casualties and was only won due to the incredible bravery of the U.S. soldiers. They had formed the most significant part of the fighting force, although over 50,000 British soldiers and some Canadians also took part. On January 25th 1945, when the Battle of the Bulge was finally over, the Allies continued their march toward Berlin. The Soviet forces reached the beleaguered German capital before them and launched their assault on the City on April 16th.

On May 2nd, after seventeen days of bitter fighting, the Battle of Berlin ended. As the Red Army closed in on him, Hitler, who had taken refuge in an underground bomb shelter below the Reich Chancellery, took his own life on 30th April. Two days before he died, his fascist dictator counterpart in Italy, Benito Mussolini and his mistress were executed by Italian partisans in Giuliano di Mezzegra.

The war in Europe was finally over, and the Instrument of Surrender was signed on May 7th at the Supreme Headquarters of the Allied Expeditionary force in the French city of Rheims.

However, the war in the Pacific raged on until finally, in August 1945, in a desperate effort to end the hostilities, the Americans dropped two atomic bombs, one on Hiroshima and the other on Nagasaki. After the bombs fell, the Japanese finally surrendered, and in Tokyo Bay, on September 2nd 1945, their Instrument of Surrender was signed on board the battleship USS Missouri.

World War II was finally over.

Chapter 21

After the end of the war, I had my mother to myself for ten happy years. She was very loving, and I cherish the time we spent together. We would visit many lovely places, and my first memory is of being taken to Longleat House, the first private stately home to open to the public. Although I was only 6 at the time, I remember how beautiful it was and how tall the Marquis of Bath seemed when he bent down and autographed my guidebook. We went on exciting holidays to Billy Butlin's Skegness and Clacton holiday camps, where my friends and I would go roller skating and swimming while my mother and her friends went in for the Fancy Dress and Miss Butlin's competitions. They were halcyon days, and many of the redcoats, whose job it was to keep us happy, became household names:

Dave Allen, Des O'Connor, and Roy Hudd, to name just a few.

When I was 5, I became a pupil at Locksheath County Primary School, which had an appropriately named head called Miss Stern. Memories of my days there are mostly happy ones, as on warm sunny days, we'd take our sewing lessons sitting under the large crab apple tree in the school grounds or go out on nature walks to pick wildflowers to take home and press in our exercise books. Our headmistress was also the music teacher; she would arrive in the classroom dressed dramatically in black silk from head to toe, then proceed to conduct our singing by manically flailing her arms around and swinging her head from side to side. We found it hard to stifle our giggles as her exaggerated movements caused straggly strands of her grey, wiry hair to flop about all over the place and escape from her elastic headband.

In the 50s, we all had a daily bottle of milk as many children were nutritionally deficient due to the deprivations of the war. School dinners were unappetizing, but occasionally the most delicious dessert, called Gypsy tart, made with evaporated milk, butter, eggs and sugar, would be dished out to us by a jolly dinner lady called Mrs Skinner. It wasn't exactly a healthy pudding, but in those days, with figures for childhood obesity very low, that wasn't an important consideration.

When I was 10, due to a quirk of fate, my mother met a gentleman coincidentally also called Ronald. He was playing the leading man in the production of a local amateur dramatic society when his opposite number fell pregnant. The producer, scouting around for a replacement, auditioned my mother, and as soon as Ronald laid eyes on his new romantic lead, it was love at first sight. She had, by that time, grown even more beautiful and had the same lovely long brown wavy hair, which I loved to brush and sprinkle with gold dust from a little glass bottle. She also enjoyed doing people's hair, but her tonsorial abilities were called into question when she used metal curlers to give my grandmother a perm. I don't think Violet ever forgave her daughter when her beautiful silvery white hair turned a bright shade of green.

My mother and Ronald had a blissfully happy marriage which produced two sons, one born three years after the other. I loved helping to bathe them and enjoyed smothering them all over with Johnson's baby powder; to this day, the smell of it brings back memories of those happy times. My mother and stepfather were fortunate

Joan's wedding to Ronald Peaple 1955 Locksheath congregational church

to have in me a built-in babysitter, allowing them to continue their love affair with amateur dramatics. My mother was an excellent actress, and I always went to see her performances. She was perfect in "Sailor Beware" as Emma Hornet, the character played by the redoubtable Peggy Mount in the film version of the play. The members of their drama group at Bitterne Park Congregational Church were friendly and sociable, and I know from what my mother told me that her time spent with them brought a lot of happiness and joy into her and Ronald's lives.

There were moments throughout her marriage when something would remind her of my father, and she would rush up the stairs in tears and shut herself away in the bedroom. My stepfather took these episodes in his stride with compassion and understanding until she emerged from the room smiling and happy once again.

Although she adored and lavished affection on her two sons, she always ensured she spent quality time with me. We would play crib together when I came home from school for my lunch break, with Workers Playtime blaring out on the radio, or we would relax on our deckchairs together in the garden on a sunny day. Such dreaded domestic tasks as helping her with the washing and wiping up were made bearable by listening to the Navy Lark, Take it from Here, Ray's a Laugh and Hancock's Half Hour on the radio.

I am so grateful to have had such kind and caring grandparents as Violet and Bill, who loved and looked after me so devotedly, and I'm also thankful to have had such a wonderful stepfather. He was humorous, good-natured and extremely kind and would spend hours patiently helping me with my homework. I can honestly say that, even in my stroppy teenage years, I hardly ever had a cross word with him. His full name was Ronald Peaple, and in his younger days, he joined the RAF, but his ambition to become a pilot had been thwarted by the discovery he was colour-blind. After his initial disappointment, he became a carpenter joiner and timber technologist, and when he and my mother married, he worked very hard to provide for us all. A popular and much-loved man, he was still leading ramblers' walks in the New Forest and playing badminton well into his 80's; as a testament to him, when he died aged 93, over 100 people attended his funeral.

Sadly, my beautiful mother enjoyed only ten years of marriage to him and died of breast cancer when she was just 40. We were all heartbroken to lose her, and not a day goes by when I don't think of her; however, I have always felt a deep sense of gratitude to my stepfather for giving her those ten blissfully happy years. It was a deep sadness to us all that she never saw her adored boys grow up, and if she had, she would have been delighted to see what remarkable young men they became.

The eldest son, Ian, was discovered to have perfect pitch and a prodigious talent for music. After enlisting into the Royal Artillery and serving in Larkhill and Germany, he took a three-year bandmaster's course at Kneller Hall, the Royal Military School of Music, where he was awarded the Worshipful Company of Musicians Silver Medal as Top Student. After this, his career took off, and he became Bandmaster of the Albuhera Band in Germany and, later, of the Black Watch in Hong Kong. After his commission, his appointment at Kneller Hall as Foundation Course Director saw him assuming responsibility for training recruits for the Corps of Army Music. His final appointment was Director

A young Mike and Ian Peaple in uniform

of Music of the Band of the Corps of REME (the Royal Electrical and Mechanical Engineers), the band he would bring to Romsey to help raise funds for the Southampton-based charity Leukaemia Busters and also to help save Romsey Hospital from closing. In 2002, a few years before he 'soldiered on' serving in the Territorial Army in Exeter and Sandhurst, he was promoted to Major. He has three children and three grandchildren, and although now separated from his delightful wife, Victoria, they remain close friends and both dote on their much-loved family.

Michael had a rewarding career in the RAF, and it would be accurate to say that Air Traffic Control was a significant part of his life. On June 12th 1987, he received a personal commendation from his Commanding Officer in conjunction with a mention in the Queen's Birthday Honours

List. A letter from his Group Captain said, "I very warmly congratulate you on this very fine achievement which recognises your outstanding contribution to the Royal Air Force West Drayton over several years. You have set an excellent example to your fellow assistants". Michael was a Flight Sergeant and served on several RAF bases during his career, including Prestwick and Cottesmore. As a natural progression, after he retired, he joined NATS, the National Air Traffic Services at Swanwick in Hampshire, an establishment that provides air traffic control services for aircraft at the U.K.'s biggest airports and to planes flying through U.K. airspace. Sadly, to the family's great sorrow, Michael died almost two years ago. Of the three of us, he was the one most like our mother; inheriting her sparkling blue eyes, winning smile and charismatic personality, and he could

Ronald Peaple with his 2 sons Ian and Mike

Mike and Fran's daughter Lisa with their grandson Freddie

Ian and Victoria's son Alexander and daughters Sophie and Emily

Ian and Victoria's grandchildren, Florence and Oscar

light up a room just by walking into it. A true family man, he had a lovely wife, Fran, with whom he had the happiest of marriages, a beautiful daughter, Lisa, and a much-loved grandson, Freddie. They all gave him so much joy during his lifetime.

I was less clever and less successful career-wise than my brothers, but loving books, I spent many happy years as a librarian. Later, I worked in the Civil Service and finally ended my working life as a Witness Support volunteer. However, like my grandmother, I enjoyed fundraising and after my husband died from leukaemia, and Sean, the five year old grandson of dear family friends died from a rare form of cancer, I began, in a small way, raising money for research into the disease. My first effort was a concert performed by the very talented members of the Southampton Musical Society. Their memorable

Ian and Victoria's grandaughter Gracie

Sean Robb grandson of Alan's oldest friend Derek Robb, another submariner. Sadly Sean died from cancer aged five

ST JAMES'S PALACE
LONDON SW1A 1BS

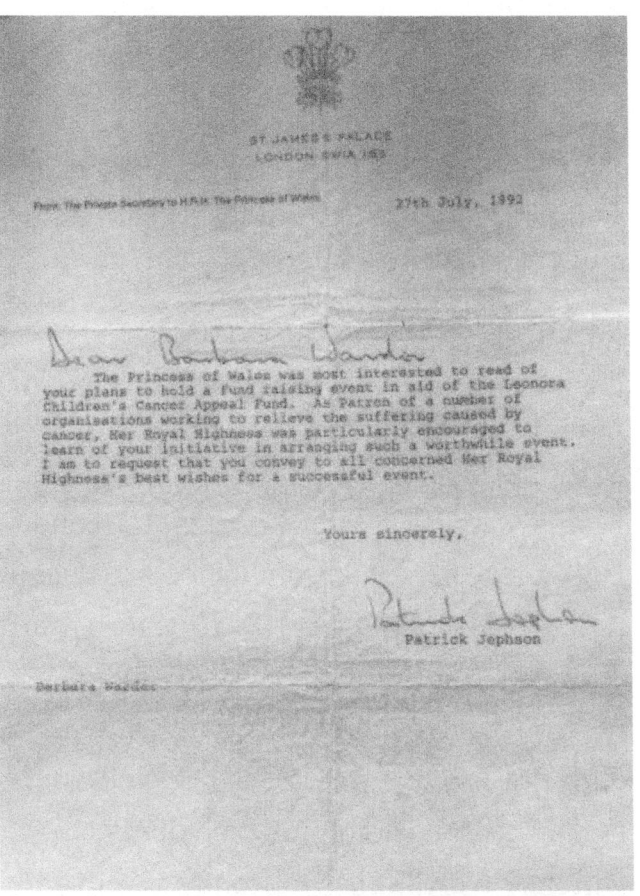

From: The Private Secretary to H.R.H. The Princess of Wales   27th July, 1992

Dear Barbara Warder

The Princess of Wales was most interested to read of your plans to hold a fund raising event in aid of the Leonora Children's Cancer Appeal Fund. As Patron of a number of organisations working to relieve the suffering caused by cancer, Her Royal Highness was particularly encouraged to learn of your initiative in arranging such a worthwhile event. I am to request that you convey to all concerned Her Royal Highness's best wishes for a successful event.

Yours sincerely,

Patrick Jephson

Barbara Warder

Letter from the late HRH Princess of Wales sending her best wishes for Leonora Children's Cancer Appeal Fund concert

performances over four nights raised over £2000 for the Leonora Cancer Trust, the charity founded by Countess Mountbatten in memory of her beloved five-year-old daughter who died from kidney cancer. I will never forget how enthusiastically the singers and dancers in SMS gave up a great deal of their time for all the necessary rehearsals and performances. It was entirely due to them that such a sizeable amount of money was raised for Leonora's charity.

Many years later, after I met my husband, Bob, I was invited to join the committee to raise funds to save Romsey Hospital from closure. Working with the much-loved Man of Romsey, Dr John White and his wife Grace, was a real privilege. The weekly meetings at the committee members' various lovely homes in Romsey were lively and enjoyable as new ideas to raise money were bounced around the room. I was constantly amazed by the innovative ideas the local people of the town and the surrounding areas came up with to boost the charity's funds, and I remember how delighted we all were when the £1,000,000 was reached.

My brother, Ian, played his part in helping the project when he brought the REME band to the town. He conducted two wonderful musical evenings: one solely for the Hospital Appeal Fund, the other jointly for the Hospital and Leukaemia Busters. The first was held at the Crosfield Hall in Romsey and the second in the grounds of Catherine and Richard Steel's beautiful home in Whiteparish in Wiltshire. As well as generously offering to hold the concert in her home, Catherine, herself a prodigious fundraiser, helped considerably with its organisation. It was a truly magical evening as a receptive audience enjoyed the strains of the beautiful music of Strauss, Tchaikovsky, Rimsky Korsakov, and

THE BAND OF
THE CORPS OF

ROYAL ELECTRICAL
&
MECHANICAL ENGINEERS

presents a Concert in aid of
Leukaemia Busters and
The Romsey Hospital Appeal

at The Granary, Whiteparish
(By kind permission of Richard & Catherine Steel)

Saturday 7th July 2001
7.30 p.m.

Rossini as they drifted over the Wiltshire countryside.

I have visited my father's grave in the Bayeux War Cemetery many times, and it always fills me with great sadness to see the thousands of headstones stretching in all directions as far as the eye can see. There are 4648 soldiers buried there, and it also has a memorial to commemorate 1808 soldiers from the Commonwealth who died in the Battle of Normandy but had no known graves.

On visiting the landing beaches, the incredible D-Day museum, and Lingèvres, where my father fell, I was occasionally accompanied by close French friends from Carpiquet and Authie, the places mentioned in Chapter 18. My husband Bob and his close friend Robin Oliver were founding members of the North Baddesley Twinning Association which was twinned with these two French villages. Over the years we have enjoyed fabulous times with our very special friends from this beautiful area of Northern France.

Sometimes it feels as if fate drew me to this Calvados region of Normandy, a place where I can truly feel close to the father I loved but never knew.

Ronald's final resting place in the Bayeux War Cemetery

My thanks go to the following people who have helped me in the writing of this book.

Mr James Delahaye (a.k.a. Ernest): for his proofreading, practical assistance and support and especially for giving me the original idea of writing my parents' love story.

Mr James Bennett: for warmly encouraging me in my efforts and especially for his invaluable help with my military research.

Mrs Vivienne Moore: for her proofreading and special thanks for her unstinting encouragement and support.

Ms Olivier Belot of Carpiquet: for his help with my French research and, again, for his much-appreciated interest in my book.

Mr Vic Green: for his excellent website vandwdestroyer.org.uk, a treasure trove of information for me; thanks to him also for patiently answering all my queries about HMS Worcester.

Mr Bob Hunt: for access to his marvellous website portsdown-tunnels.org.uk, which provided me with an important and unique source of information.

Rtd Wing Commander John Lambert: special thanks for the benefit of his RAF expertise and for his, as always, warm encouragement.

The late Mr Derek Robb: for his memories of life as a submariner with his dear friend Alan Potter. Derek was the grandfather of Sean, one of the children this book was written in memory of.

Rtd Commander Nick La Hive: for sharing his memories of his maritime career with his dear friend Alan Potter and, as always, for his kindness and support to me.

Mr Mark Averiss. Chairman of Falmouth Cricket Club: for all his help with details of the Hawkey connection to his excellent Club at Trescobeas. May your next season be very successful.

Miss Jane Painter, archivist of St Nicholas Church: for her help concerning details of my Father's memorial in the beautiful church in Wickham.

Last but by no means least, to my darling husband Bob, who has been an enormous help to me throughout the time I have been working on this book. He has provided me with invaluable practical and emotional support for the past two years.

Printed in Great Britain
by Amazon